AFRICAN IMAGES

AFRICAN

Pictures
by
Ugo Mochi

Text by
Dorcas MacClintock

IMAGES

CHARLES SCRIBNER'S SONS • NEW YORK

Quotes on pages 54 and 115 reprinted with permission of Macmillan Publishing Company from *The Long African Day* by Norman Myers. Copyright © 1972 by Norman Myers.

Quotes on pages 2, 51, and 71 from *Out of Africa* by Isak Dinesen. Copyright 1937 by Random House, Inc. and renewed 1965 by Rungstedlundfonden. Reprinted by permission of the publisher.

Quotes on pages 46–47 and 50 from *East African Mammals,* volumes IIIB and IIIC, by Jonathan Kingdon. Reprinted by permission of Academic Press, Inc., Ltd., London, England.

Illustrations on pages xiii, 39, 65, 103, 105, 133, 134, 136 (top), 137, and 139 from *A Natural History of Zebras* by Dorcas MacClintock and Ugo Mochi. Text copyright © 1976 Dorcas MacClintock. Illustrations copyright © 1976 Ugo Mochi. Reprinted by permission of Charles Scribner's Sons.

Illustrations on pages 6 (bottom), 7, 10 (bottom), 12 (bottom), 49, 64, 115, and 136 (bottom) from *Hoofed Mammals of the World* by Dorcas MacClintock and Ugo Mochi. Text and illustrations copyright 1953 by Ugo Mochi and T. Donald Carter; renewed 1981 by Edna Mochi, Joanne Mochi Gray, and Jeanne Mochi Tartaglia. Reprinted by permission of Charles Scribner's Sons.

Illustrations on pages 52, 54, and 72 (bottom) from *A Natural History of Giraffes* by Dorcas MacClintock and Ugo Mochi. Text copyright © 1973 Dorcas MacClintock. Illustrations copyright © 1973 Ugo Mochi. Reprinted by permission of Charles Scribner's Sons.

Text copyright © 1984 Dorcas MacClintock
Illustrations copyright © 1984 Estate of Ugo Mochi

Library of Congress Cataloging in Publication Data
Mochi, Ugo, 1889–   African images.
Includes bibliographical references and index.
Summary: Animal silhouettes with accompanying text present the characteristics and habits of the animals of Africa.
1. Zoology—Africa. [1. Zoology—Africa.   2. Africa]
I. MacClintock, Dorcas.   II. Title.
QL336.M58   1984   591.96   84-10565
ISBN 0-684-18089-8

1   3   5   7   9   11   13   15   17   19   Q/C   20   18   16   14   12   10   8   6   4   2

Printed in the United States of America

To Ugo Mochi's daughters
Jeanne and Joanne

Contents

Acknowledgments

I am most grateful to the family of the late Ugo Mochi for making this book possible: to Edna Mochi, his wife, for her support and enthusiasm; and especially to Jeanne Mochi Tartaglia, his daughter, who did so much of the work in selecting and preparing the artwork for photographing.

To my mother, Helen Kay Eason, whose death came as this manuscript was being finished, my debt is enormous. She opened my eyes to a world filled with beauty, in books and in art, as well as in animals.

Photographers Lou Carol Lecce, of Albany, New York, William K. Sacco, of Yale Peabody Museum, and Bill Meng, of the New York Zoological Park, deserve thanks for their skill and care in photographing the original cutouts, too delicate to send to the printer.

Among those who kindly loaned original artwork for inclusion in the book are: The New York Zoological Society (greater kudu group), Mr. and Mrs. Albert E. Gilbert (forest elephant and giant eland), Dr. and Mrs. Brian Quinn (sable antelope), and Mr. and Mrs. Gregory Finkell (lion pride).

I would also thank William Gruenerwald, whose concern for zebras and their rhinoceros relatives is unbounded, for sharing recent information on the status of white rhinos in the Sudan.

Again I have relied on the Kline Science Library at Yale University, a refuge as well as a storehouse of zoological information, and its ever-helpful staff of reference librarians.

Finally I would like to give special thanks to all those observers of African animal life on whose insights I have drawn in writing a text to accompany Ugo Mochi's African images.

—*Dorcas MacClintock*

Prologue

Africa has an extraordinary diversity of animal life. Variations of terrain and climate produce *habitats*★ that range from lush mountain forests, to forest-margin communities, to wooded *savannas,* to open grasslands, to arid bushlands. Some species—isolated during geologic time as changes in climate and rainfall caused moist forests and dry savannas to transgress and regress across the continent—remain restricted to scattered forest areas. Many animals have adapted to living on the plains or in the arid bush. Still others inhabit wooded savannas or live along rivers or in swamps and marshes.

Although zebras, giraffes, lions, and other spectacular animals were seen in the circuses of Rome in the second century A.D., the first accounts of Africa's animals came from early explorer-naturalists. By the turn of the last century, sportsmen and big-game hunters also were writing of their adventures. On a more scientific level, museum parties went afield to collect skeletons and hides.

In the 1940s and 1950s, growing concern for the animals and their environment led to the creation of national parks and reserves. By the 1960s, scientists from Germany, Britain, Canada, and the United States were carrying on field studies. At first the emphasis was on

---

★Italicized words are defined in the glossary (pages 147–150).

numbers, distribution, habitats, and population dynamics (most mammals maintain a population level that is in equilibrium with their habitat; sometimes there is an increase, sometimes a decrease in the ever-shifting balance between birth and death). Then *ethologists* (scientists who study the behavior of animals) began to focus attention on the social organization, behavior, and ecology of particular mammal species.

Present-day field studies involve the collecting of detailed data on individual animals—recognized by spot or stripe patterns, ear notches, scars, or by marking or radio-collaring—and systematic sampling techniques. Behavior observations are recorded for a given length of time on special data sheets and later quantified by computer analysis. In many instances the ethologist concentrates on a single aspect of behavior, such as patterns of social grouping, relations within the group (herd, pack, band, or troop), dominance hierarchy (the structure within the group), territoriality (the tendency of some animals to defend an area against other individuals of the same species), mother-infant relations, or play behavior.

Nowhere on earth is beauty of animal form, modeled through time by physical function and environment, so apparent. Hoofed mammals, always watchful for *predators,* reveal tension in the brightness of an eye, the alert stance, the poise of a head on the curve of neck, the stamp of a forefoot, or the whisk of a tail. Predators, too, are tense as they stalk, wait in ambush, or sprint after their *prey.* At other times they loll about in the heat of the day.

There is beauty of color as well as of form. Patterns have evolved on some animals—stripes, splotches, and spots—that break up body outlines or provide camouflage. Other animals have conspicuous markings on face, ears, or legs that function for recognition among their own kind, emphasize mood or intent, or are flaunted in displays of dominance between rivals.

Perhaps the most beautiful of the hoofed mammals, or *ungulates,* are the antelopes in all their variety of sizes, body contours, and horn shapes. All of them are *bovids,* members of the family Bovidae, which also includes the gazelles and the African buffalo. Originally forest an-

imals, some of the antelopes remain forest or forest-margin inhabitants. A number of antelopes are *browsers* in bush country. Many others have adapted for living out on the plains as grazers.

Birds as well as mammals are part of the African scene and its wide range of landscapes. On wind-ruffled lakes pelicans sail in graceful flotillas. Along lake shores water birds and plains birds intermingle. Forest fringes contain birds of both forest and savanna.

In Africa, watching animals becomes a preoccupation. Early morning and late afternoon are times for looking at them. Then, in half light, their body forms are outlined to appear as images, sculptured likenesses of the animals themselves.

xiv   AFRICAN IMAGES

1 The Forests

Most of Africa's mountain peaks are the cones or craters of ancient volcanoes. Some cones still steam or actively spew lava; most of them, including Kilimanjaro, the highest mountain in Africa, and the towering peaks of mounts Kenya and Elgon, are extinct. Ngorongoro, its grassland floor teeming with animals, is a volcanic crater.

The mist-shrouded Ruwenzori range that separates Uganda and Zaire is not volcanic. Its peaks, some covered by snow and glaciers, project in groups from a massive block of rock heaved up when the Rift Valley was formed.

On the mountains, rainfall differences create zones of vegetation. In alpine areas, just below snowline, only mosses and lichens grow; in boggy moorlands, giant plants thrive; bamboo forests give way downslope to montane forests. These mountain forest communities, remnants of forests that once covered much of Africa, are widely separated by vast stretches of savanna and grassland.

In the struggle upward for sunlight giant hardwood trees and tall, nonflowering evergreens tower above a canopy formed by the tops of smaller trees. Creepers, beards of lichens, and other epiphytes (plants that grow on trees) flourish in high humidity. Where shafts of light penetrate, bracken and wild bananas form thickets, and grasses grow in open glades. Much of the dark forest floor is carpeted by a thick layer of leaf mold.

The forest is a mysterious place, likened by the writer Isak Dinesen to an old tapestry "darkened with age but marvellously rich in green shades," a place where "you cannot see the sky at all . . . , but the sunlight plays in many strange ways, falling through the foliage."★

Bird sounds fill the air. Raucous calls that carry half a mile are interspersed with faint, bell-like sounds that scarcely reach the forest floor. The birds themselves are hard to see. Turacos flash red or violet and green in the canopy and sound their croaking calls. Mousebirds climb and run among the branches, their long, ten-feathered tails downcurved like those of mice. The mammals of the forest are secretive, often nocturnal, and harder still to see.

Bongo

One of these elusive animals is the bongo. Largest of the forest antelopes, it is deep chestnut-red. Some older males are almost black. Enormous, bold-patterned ears detect the slightest sound. The bongo belongs to the *tragelaphines,* a group of exceptionally beautiful antelopes that have narrow heads, spiral or twisted horns, a dorsal crest of hairs, and vertical white stripes on their flat-sided bodies. Like many of the tragelaphines, the bongo has black-and-white markings on its legs.

Bongos are browsers of forest glades and elephant-tangle thickets (low vegetation maintained by the browsing activity of elephants). Isolated populations of bongos live on Mount Kenya, in the Aberdares, and in the Mau ranges. Bongos also occur in a narrow forest stretch from Sierra Leone to southwestern Sudan, where three small reserves have been established primarily for bongos.

Bongos rely on dense cover for protection. Their body stripes merge with narrow patterns of sunlight to make their antelope outlines almost invisible. In fact, bongos are virtual forest ghosts. When glimpsed at all, they are screened by undergrowth and vines. Once a bongo scents danger, it freezes. Then, breaking cover, it vanishes as

---

★Isak Dinesen,*Out of Africa* (New York, Random House, 1970), p.64.

though by magic. It dashes through the undergrowth, head low and spiral horns laid back on the neck, their tips rubbing the antelope's shoulders.

During most of the day bongos rest and ruminate (chew cud). In late afternoon they emerge from dense cover to forage for bamboo shoots, stinging nettles, roots, rotting wood, and to feed in open glades. In the Aberdare Mountains the Kikuyu and Luo tribespeople's habit of shifting cultivation areas often benefits the bongo when lush secondary growth reinvades abandoned garden plots. But people also threaten the bongo by snaring them along forest paths or trailing them with dogs and spears. To eat the meat of the red-striped antelope once was thought to cause leprosy, a disease that, untreated, causes lesions and deformities. As human populations now crowd the bongo's forest refuges, it is no longer protected by such tribal taboos.

3   The Forests

Its continuing existence depends on strict government protection.

Bongos are predictable visitors at The Ark and Treetops, safari lodges where salt licks attract animals for nighttime viewing. Bongos

also are fond of wallowing in mud, after which they vigorously rub body and horns against tree trunks.

Bulls lead a solitary life. Occasional forest encounters sometimes result in a sparring match. Necks swell, horns are held in vertical position, and eyes roll in a visual *display* that usually precludes a fight. Females, associated loosely in small groups, usually under the leadership of an old cow, are continually watched by the wandering bulls. At calving time, a cow goes off by herself. Her tawny calf will lie hidden for a month or so until it is old enough to join a nursery herd of other cows and their calves. Vulnerable to leopards, pythons, and hyenas, the calf has some protection in the herd, where a leopard's ambush may be met with lowered head and a horn-skewering defensive charge.

Duiker

In Afrikaans *duiker* means "diver" and refers to this small antelope's way of diving through the underbrush. Not quite two feet tall, the duiker has a low-slung body on slender legs, forequarters shorter than the hind ones, a wedge-shaped head, back-slanted horns, and large eyes, all of which are adaptations for furtive forest life. So characteristic of forest habitat are the duikers that all the isolated forests of Africa have at least one species of these hunchbacked little antelopes, most of them reddish or brownish in color.

The duiker is a forest-floor browser, feeding on seeds, shoots, leaves, bark, and roots. Now and then it picks up a large fruit dropped by monkeys overhead, shifting the juicy delicacy about in its large mouth. Craving minerals and especially salt, which is hard to find in humid forests, the duiker sometimes eats insects and even carrion.

Picking its way through the forest with high, dainty steps, the duiker stops now and again to snuffle in the leaves. When alarmed it gives a harsh, sneezing whistle and dashes off. Within its *home range,* trails connect feeding, ruminating, and resting places. *Territory* is defined by the male. He stands or rests in certain places and he marks,

with secretion from the conspicuous maxillary gland on each side of his face. Glandular marking is also important when duikers meet. Although duikers are not gregarious and, like most of the small antelopes, move about singly or in pairs, they sometimes enjoy mutual grooming sessions, when one duiker licks another's forehead hair tuft and nuzzles its head and shoulders.

Okapi

In the dense, damp, and dark equatorial forests of northeastern Zaire lives the elegant okapi. Almost five feet at the shoulders, this compact-bodied *ungulate* (hoofed mammal) has a velvety dark chestnut,

chocolate-brown, or purplish-black coat. Females are redder and somewhat larger than males. Only males have small, hair-covered horns. Like its close relative, the giraffe, the okapi has a sloping back. Although it is not as tall as a giraffe, the okapi splays its forelegs to drink from a forest stream. In fact, the okapi resembles an extinct short-necked ancestral giraffe, a fossil form called *Paleotragus* that lived some ten million years ago in Eurasia.

Transverse black-on-white stripes mark the okapi's hindquarters. Its legs have wide black bands. Yet in its forest habitat this large animal is almost impossible to find. Until 1901 the okapi was unknown to science. To be sure, there had been hints of its existence. Explorer Sir Henry Morton Stanley had been told by Mbuti tribespeople that there were "horses" much like the ones he rode in the Ituri forest. Some years later, Sir Harry Johnston, governor of the Uganda protectorate, pursued this animal the Mbuti called "o'api." He acquired several bandoliers or belts made from black-and-white rump skin of

what at first was thought to be a new kind of zebra. Then hoofprints of a large two-toed ungulate were found. Although Johnston returned to his Uganda post without seeing the okapi, he later received a parcel containing the skin and two skulls of the animal that had eluded him. When the okapi was described in a scientific journal it was named *Okapia johnstoni* in honor of the governor.

The okapi has enormous, broad ears and acute hearing. Its eyes are large and dark. It has a very long, bluish-gray *prehensile* tongue, a useful browsing tool that it wraps around buds, leaves, or twigs, pulling

them into its mouth. The tongue is also used, like a wet washcloth, for grooming face and body.

During downpours okapis seek shelter under dense forest growth. There are favorite places, glades and small valleys, for daytime browsing. Okapi pathways through the forest are marked by hoof-gland secretion and by urine. The okapi is often solitary. Pairs form during courtship. Occasionally a small family group is glimpsed.

Because mating is a matter of chance, the female okapi's *estrus* (period of being "in heat") lasts several weeks. She advertises her readiness for mating with plaintive trumpeting calls. Bull and cow consort for days and even weeks, with repeated matings during the courtship.

Some fourteen months later, at a time of year when rainfall is heaviest, the calf is born. It has a small head and stocky legs, and its almost-black coat is much darker than its mother's. A wispy mane extends down its spine from head to tail. For a time it lies hidden in underbrush, maintaining contact with its mother by bleating and whistling calls. Soon it trails its mother through the forest, always within sight of her bold rump pattern of black spokes on white.

Drill

Mandrill and drill, close relatives of the baboons, live in forests of West Africa. They roam among trees, search for edible plants, dig for roots, and eat mice and other small animals. Large adult males have harems of five to ten females and their young. The mandrill has a brilliant blue-and-red face. The drill's face, except for a red chin, is black. Both of these powerfully built monkeys have vividly colored rumps and upright tail stubs.

African Porcupine

At dusk or after dark, the porcupine leaves its comfortable burrow system to waddle along a familiar forest path. This largest of African rodents is stout bodied, long legged, and nearly three feet tall at the top of its quilled back. A crest of slender, back-curved bristles covers its head and neck. Over its back are hollow, sharp-pointed, lightly rooted, and easily detached quills. Each foot-long quill is banded black, brown, and white. Almost obscured among the hindquarter quills is a short tail.

As though aware of the safety its armor insures, the porcupine rattles noisily as it moves. It pauses to dig for roots and bulbs or to eat bark, berries, and fruits. Like most rodents, it craves minerals and gnaws on bones or even elephant tusks whenever it comes upon them.

When the porcupine encounters another forest animal, it erects and violently rattles its quills, a display that usually deters an aggressor. If the aggressor presses on, the porcupine twists around, spreads wide its heavy body quills, shivers its tail, stamps its forefeet, and jerks backward to quill the persistent predator.

Giant Forest Hog

The largest of the living pigs is a forest dweller. Unlike its savanna-scrub relative, the warthog, the giant forest hog tends to be *nocturnal*. It has a massive snout, small, pointed ears, and coarse almost-black hair. Scattered small populations are found in mountain forests and forest-savanna areas, often near abandoned farm plots. Dense undergrowth and tangles of fallen trees are used for shelter. So are shallow caves, which are excavated with the hog's flat, forward-projecting incisor teeth in road or stream banks. Actually these sleeping places are dormitories, for *sounders* (family groups) like to sleep communally, all heaped together in a pile. Favorite rubbing trees, dung sites, and mineral licks also mark giant hog habitat.

A sow and her offspring—as many as several generations—sometimes accompanied by a large boar, form a sounder. In this basic social unit of the pig family the little piglets follow their mother in tight formation. They depend on her ability to detect the approach of leopard or hyenas, and if a boar is present, they have still better protection. Like their elders, young hogs have a broad, flat muzzle and a bare nose patch or *rhinarium*. They prepare for adult skirmishes by playful bouts of snout-knocking.

Mature boars, much larger than females, tend to avoid each other. When a confrontation does occur, they match foreheads and shove or back off, manes bristled, to charge and clash heads. Froth speckles their bodies as the noisy contest continues until one boar turns tail, conceding defeat.

Bongo frequent the small grassy clearings that are grazing places for giant hog sounders. Occasionally a bongo is mobbed by a sounder. Snouts out and sniffing, the hogs circle the antelope. When one of them moves in for a closer sniff, the bongo bounds away, hogs in pursuit. Or the bongo may turn on a too-bold hog and strike at it with lowered head. Then, squealing, the hog flees.

Forest Buffalo

The open grassy areas along rivers, in boggy areas, and in small clearings used by giant hogs and bongo are called buffalo glades. They are maintained by the grazing and browsing of small groups of forest buffaloes. Smaller and lighter-horned than their African or Cape buffalo relative, forest buffalo bulls are dark reddish brown, the cows yellowish red in color. They graze in glades, browse forest fringes, seek out abundant mud for wallowing, and move into the forest for shelter.

Water Chevrotain

Along forest streams and swamps lives a tiny-hoofed animal, a primitive ruminant thought to look much like the common ancestor of the deer and giraffe families and the bovids (cattle and antelopes). The water chevrotain is rich brown in color and has a white side stripe and several rows of white body spots. Its head is small, with a pointed nose, used for pushing through vegetation, and rounded ears. Its hunched back is protected by a thick layer of dermal muscles, a shield against thorns and sharp twigs. It has delicate, pencil-thin legs and a short tail.

The chevrotain's feet are piglike, with four (rather than two) well-developed digits on each foot. Because the animal stands on toe tip, the lateral toes do not touch ground. Males have small, curved, tusk-like upper canine teeth that protrude below the lips. In fights they rush at each other with open mouths and slashing teeth.

At night the chevrotain feeds on fallen fruits, aquatic plants, lily roots, and grass. Sometimes it eats aquatic animals, insects, and crabs, or scavenges fish. During the day it may leave its form, or resting place, to climb up a sloping tree trunk or onto a tangle of vines. If a predator appears, the chevrotain dashes off with rabbitlike jumps. Water is its refuge. Plunging in, the chevrotain swims upstream a short way to emerge beneath a protective overhang of bank vegetation.

Gorilla

A gorilla's life is leisurely. Being a terrestrial ape, it moves on all fours, the soles of its hind feet and the knuckles of its hands support-ing its weight. The gorilla *troop* files from place to place, now and again pausing to feed. As they disperse, searching for food, the goril-las maintain contact by grunting. Heads turned sideways and corner-of-the-eye glances give reassurance among troop members. The gorillas sit or stand on three legs, using their free hands to snatch vegetation. Stems of wild celery, shoots and pith of tree ferns, and leaves and blossoms of various plants make up the vegetarian diet of these gentle creatures.

A troop consists of five to twenty or more individuals. Usually there are two or three silverbacks (older males), a few blackback males, eight or more females, and a varying number of juveniles and infants.

Except for the come-and-go status of the males, the troop has a fairly constant composition. When troops meet, the silverbacks en-gage in an emotional exchange—self-assertion, threat, and challenge. Hooting is followed by displacement activities of leaf-snatching and eating. This behavior gives way to the tearing up of vegetation, then chest-beating and leg-kicking. They make sideways dashes on all fours, slap at the undergrowth, and thump the ground with their palms. This ritualized display is watched with interest by the other males.

At dusk nests are made, beds of bent bamboo or branches broken off to form body-size, saucerlike depressions. A few of the younger gorillas may climb trees to make their nests.

Once they are six to eight months old and big enough to leave their mothers' arms, young gorillas are full of play. Sometimes their antics try the patience of other troop members. Ethologist George Schaller observed a ten-month-old gorilla attempt, by hair pulling, to get a rise out of a juvenile. The tolerant young gorilla did not respond. Finally the infant gave up and, rolling over, arms and legs flailing, turned over and over downslope to disappear in the underbrush.

Gorillas are found on the Virunga Mountain slopes bordering Rwanda and Zaire and in the Bwindi forest area of southwestern Uganda. In 1960 it was estimated that 450 gorillas lived on the slopes of the Virunga Mountains. A 1982 census shows 240 gorillas in Rwanda and about 120 gorillas remaining in the Bwindi forest, some 25 miles to the north. Human encroachment drives the gentle apes higher and higher up the mountains. As land is cleared for planting and wood cut for fuel to support a population that grows at a rate of more than 4 percent a year, loss of habitat will ultimately threaten the gorilla's survival. For the time being Rwanda keeps careful watch over the gorilla groups that remain and guards them from poachers.

Chimpanzee

Africa's smaller ape makes its home in the Budongo Forest of western Uganda and forest areas in western Tanzania, including the Gombe Stream Reserve (now a national park), where Jane Goodall continues her study of chimpanzee behavior begun in the early 1960s.

Chimpanzees live in loosely structured groups. Troops are noisy, hooting often and beating with hands and heels on buttresses of tall trees to proclaim their territories. Usually a chimpanzee walks with hind legs flexed, body forward, and arms straight. It pauses now and then and stands upright to peer over the undergrowth or walk on its hind legs, toes turned inward.

Social rank, at least among males, appears to depend on one ape's ability to intimidate another. At Gombe, the mild-mannered, low-ranking Mike found he could take over as dominant male whenever the troop came into camp by banging two empty kerosene cans ahead of his hooting charges at the other males.

Young chimpanzees, two or three years old, spend much of the day playing. They tickle, bite, and hit each other, chase around tree trunks, and leap one after the other from branch to branch.

By nightfall chimpanzees have climbed high into trees and pulled branches to form their overnight sleeping nests.

Brush-tailed Porcupine

During the day brush-tailed porcupines shelter, often three to eight of them together, among forest tree roots or under stream banks. At night they forage together, eating leaves, bark, roots, and insects. This long-bodied rodent with a scaly, white bristle-tufted tail runs swiftly for a porcupine. It is also an agile tree climber and, having feet that are partially webbed, a good swimmer.

The *pelage* is almost entirely spiny, although on head, belly, and legs the spines are softer. Most of the body spines are flattened and grooved. Interspersed among the long lower-back spines are a number of long, round, thick quills.

2 Along Rivers

Strips of forest border large rivers. These so-called riverine forests are home to some animals that inhabit the montane forests, as well as to a host of animals particularly their own. Here and there among dense evergreen trees festooned with creeping vines, fig trees, and thick undergrowth are wide trails that lead to water. Made by elephants and hippos, they are used by many plains animals coming to drink.

Overhead, light-footed vervet monkeys, their black faces ruffed with white, leap from branch to branch, feeding on leaves, shoots, seeds, and flowers. Their alarm calls when a predator approaches elicit appropriate evasive response from the troop. If the predator is a snake or leopard, the monkeys climb higher. A different alarm call, signaling a soaring eagle, causes them to descend into the underbrush to hide.

Birds are attracted by ripening fruits. The raucous *kar* calls of brightly colored turacos, the penetrating *go-waar* of the mousebird,

and the repeated *chr-chr-chr*s of thrushlike bulbuls fills the riverine forest. At night huge fruit bats feed on figs, swallowing only the juice and rejecting the fruit fiber in pellets that patter on the forest floor.

Hornbills nest in riverine forests. Using mud and manure carried to the tree by the male hornbill, the female walls herself inside a hollow-trunk cavity. Then, throughout the long incubation period, she relies on her mate to feed her through the small opening.

Baboon

Baboons inhabit open woodland, savannas, grassland, and rocky hill country. Primarily ground dwellers, they climb into trees along thinly bushed river courses to sleep or find rock refuges on steep, wooded escarpments and atop the larger *kopjes* (islands of huge boulders). The troop sleeps, travels, and feeds as a unit. It makes long daytime foraging trips through grass and scrub. In the open, safety lies in numbers. Troops of 25 to 50 baboons sometimes associate in hordes of 100 or more.

Baboons move in a dignified manner. In the center of the troop are the big, dog-muzzled dominant males (seven or eight of them) with the females (about fifteen) and their youngest progeny. Tiny black infants cling upside down to their mothers' undersides. Older babies ride astride their mothers' backs like small jockeys. In the lead and flanking the procession are younger males, scouts and protectors.

Social organization is the secret of baboon success. Troop structure is organized around a stable core of females and their kin. Each of these females heads a *matriline* that has a shared dominance rank. Thus a small baboon in one matriline ranks above a larger individual in another, lower-ranking matriline. While adult males occasionally change from one troop to another, the females spend their lives in the troop in which they are born. Female solidarity is the basis of baboon society.

Young males leave the troop as they approach sexual maturity. They make their way into a new troop by hanging out on the periphery and making friends with one or two of the females. Accepted by them, the young male makes his way into the troop.

Among males in a troop there is also a dominance structure, but it is one that changes from time to time. Newcomer males are continually on the make. In spite of the newcomer's aggression, the resident males are more adept in social strategies. Experience and familiarity gives these established males an edge in competing for females and food.

There are also preference relationships, or friendships, formed within a troop and evidenced by two baboons feeding and moving together and by grooming. Usually a friendship involves two females, and the bond is real. In troop disputes, one female is supportive of the other and of her youngsters as well.

Now and then the troop stops, and baboons sit back on their haunches. Baboons are opportunistic feeders, eating almost anything. As they work over an area their gentle grunting sounds maintain group contact. Roots and tubers are eaten, stones are turned over in search of insect food. Sometimes a lizard is caught, or a fledgling bird, or a rodent. Less often a small monkey or a newborn gazelle hidden in the grass is a baboon's victim. Baboons are fond of meat.

Social grooming is a baboon pastime. This pleasurable act of parting and raking through the hair with hands and teeth, searching for parasites, cements ties, or bonds, between members of the troop. It also cleans their coats, ridding fur of dirt and burrs and removing ticks and scabs from the skin.

At sundown the troop climbs into a tall tree to settle for the night. Gibbering among themselves the baboons balance on their tough rump skin pads. They sleep sitting up and they sleep lightly, always alert for a leopard's climbing visit. Then hoarse alarm barks sound from the males, and the troop flees into the highest branches. Two males stay behind to confront the leopard, whose strong, curved claws hold a young baboon. Mantle hairs bristling, they grunt and screech and flash their long, pointed canine teeth.

Bushpig

Compact little pigs with tasseled ears and long, wispy tails, their snouted heads seemingly attached without necks to their flat-sided muscular bodies, bushpigs are nocturnal rooters. They live in montane and riverine forest habitats, and in marshes and swamps, places where ground is soft and vegetation is dense.

Rootling with their bone-reinforced, wedgelike skulls, they plough up soil and overturn logs. The bushpig's rhinarium, a sharp-edged disc nose pad, is used to dig, ram, and to sniffle and test by touch and smell. Tuberous roots, fallen fruits, fern rhizomes, and grass tufts are eaten. Nighttime raids are also made on cultivated crops. Elephant dung is rooted in search of beetles and larvae. Like the rest of their family, bushpigs are omnivores. They eat reptiles, birds, mammals, even carrion. They forage with competitive frenzy, all the time maintaining group contact by grunting.

Piglets are born in a thicket or in a hollow-tree nest, padded with nesting material the sow has brought in. When her three to six spotted piglets are old enough, the sow joins up with other females in a sounder of 20 or more, usually accompanied by a large boar. Bushpigs also consort in pairs, in a mother-and-piglets group, and in bachelor groups.

Rubbing, mane nibbling, and nose sparring take place among group members. Bushpigs also use tree trunks and branches as rubbing posts. Along forest trails they tusk tree trunks with their short, sharp, protruding canine teeth. Carpal (wrist) glands mark paths that connect their resting and feeding places.

When cornered by a leopard, lion, or hyena, the bushpig's defense is to erect the bristly white hairs of its mane and lower its snout. This makes its stout little body appear larger. It squeals and roars. Bushpigs have been seen to charge in and drive a leopard from its kill and then feed on the carcass.

21 Along Rivers

3 Soda Lakes and Rift Valley Walls

Alkaline lakes, some of them fed by rivers, others by hot springs, are all that remain of the swamps and lakes that once covered the floor of the Great Rift, a magnificent gash that runs half the length of Africa, from the Red Sea to the Zambesi River.

Called soda lakes, they are very rich in salts, mainly sodium bicarbonate, which are carried down by runoff from the carbonate-rich volcanic rocks of edge-of-the-Rift escarpments. Along the shores of some lakes, hot springs steam and well among the rocks to produce an inflow of soda. Many of the lakes have no outlets. They are shallow. Evaporation rate is high, often causing their perimeters to shrink. Blue-green algae and tiny one-celled plants called diatoms make a veritable broth of the highly alkaline water and give the lakes a blue-green color.

Flamingo

The souplike concentration of algae and diatoms, which is high in nutrients, is food for flamingos. Both greater and lesser flamingos are the only birds especially adapted to filter-feed on the algae. The lesser flamingo has carried this head-down sieving technique to the extreme. It feeds in huge flocks, its backward-pointing bill skimming the water of inshore shallows for the algae and diatoms that are its only food. Greater flamingos prefer deeper water (one to two feet) and are bot-

tom feeders, dipping their heads underwater for shrimp and for molluscs and other mud-dwellers.

Startled by a marabou stork, a feeding flock takes to the air in pink-and-black profusion. Long red legs and feet make loud patterings before the birds lift off to fly, high and honking, to another Rift lake.

Pelican

Pelicans fly with leisurely wingbeats and short periods of gliding. Their heads are carried back on their necks. Except for grunting croaks near the nesting colony, pelicans are silent birds. Frequently

they fly in to Rift Valley lakes where fish have been introduced for mosquito control.

The pelican is a surface fisher. Its long, rather flat upper *mandible* (beak) is hooked at the tip. The lower mandible supports a gular pouch, capacious and leathery, that is used as a landing net. Plunging its bill into the water, the pelican snatches a fish and then lets the water drain out. With a backward thrust of the head it swallows the fish.

Sometimes seven or more pelicans form a fishing party. They swim in line, in crescent formation, or paddle purposefully toward shore, beating their wings to drive the fish ahead of them. Suddenly, in one motion, their bills are plunged and the trapped fish are seized.

Marabou

This tall stork with bald pink-and-gray, scabby head and dark gray wing feathers stomps along, clacking its large bill. The marabou is the flamingo's chief enemy. It strides purposefully along the lakeshore, herding the flamingos into deeper water where their jump-and-patter-over-the-water takeoff technique is made more difficult. Suddenly the marabou takes wing and flies toward the pack of pink birds. Pandemonium results. In the confusion a flamingo, usually one in the center of the feathered crush, is pinned by the marabou. Its feathers soaked, the flamingo ceases to struggle.

Marabou predation on chicks controls flamingo populations. In the huge nesting colonies, chicks hatch within a week's time. Marabous stalk from nest to nest, paying little heed to parental protests. Chick after chick is tossed down their scrawny throats.

Crocodile nesting grounds are also monitored. Below Kabalega Falls on the Victoria Nile, marabous perch high on tree snags to wait for hatchlings to emerge. When the female crocodile is not about, they stalk the bank and probe deep into the sand to spear eggs and eat embryos.

For the most part marabous are scavengers. They stand in solemn array near the fish-processing plant at Gil Gil and loiter, naked neck pouches hanging, on the fringes of fishing villages. They feed along lakeshores on the flotsam of dead fish.

On the wing, neck retracted and legs trailing, the marabou sails in wide circles to gain height. While soaring it scans the ground and watches for vultures planing down to land at a kill.

Consorting at a carcass, the marabou stands by. Its long bill is useless for tearing flesh, so it waits for opportunities to pirate meat torn off by vultures.

Klipspringer

The rocky escarpments, often nearly vertical, that form Rift Valley walls are habitat for the klipspringer, a small antelope that, with a few ear flicks, can leap upward from a frozen stance and then ricochet from one rock surface to another as it bounds still higher. Its tiny, steep hoofs have blunt tips and are rubberlike, to prevent slipping. Its eyes are large and widely spaced and its nose, being short and wedge-shaped, allows for some degree of binocular vision that is undoubtedly useful in takeoff and landing. A klipspringer is ever alert for hawks and eagles overhead and on the watch for leopard, baboons, caracal, or serval from below.

Coarse, brittle, grayish-white hairs, each with an air-filled core, give a chunky look to the klipspringer's small body. Its method of cooling is to fluff its coat. For warmth in its often cold, high-altitude habitat, it pulls down the hairs to retain body heat.

Males are territorial. They make dung deposits and anoint bitten-off grass stems with secretion from their *preorbital* (below the inner corner of the eye) glands to mark the perimeters of their small, largely vertical territories of about seven hectares (753,000 square feet). Both sexes scent-mark in succession sometimes, a kind of communication that may lead to formation of a *pair bond*.

The newborn kid lies hidden, visited only briefly by its mother for suckling. Five weeks later it accompanies her on short, rocky forays. At three months it moves with her all the time, as agile as an adult klipspringer.

Klipspringers, usually in groups of two or three, pluck leaves from low shrubs that grow among the rocks. In the dry season when this escarpment vegetation is depleted, they move down to feed on grass and shrubs on the valley floor.

4 Swamps and Marshes

Africa's freshwater lakes support many fish-eating birds. Kingfishers dive from low, lakeside perches. Herons stalk along the shores. Fish eagles fly low in search of dead fish.

Marsh areas of bullrushes and reeds are frequented by crowned cranes, egrets, and ibises. Long-toed jacanas tread on floating rafts of lily leaves. Farther from shore, ducks and geese swim and feed.

Giant five-meter-(sixteen-foot-) high sedges, topped by flags of fine bracts, grow from thick mats of dead stems in papyrus swamps. These impenetrable tangles, land-based or floating, are the haunt of a tall, morose-looking bird with a topknot and huge, shoe-shaped bill. The whale-headed stork stands solemnly waiting to snatch a frog, turtle, or fish, while birdwatchers on safari vie for photographing positions.

29   Swamps and Marshes

Small mammals, *carnivores* and rodents, lead specialized lives in marshes. So do a few of the larger mammals. The sitatunga slinks among the reeds of some marshes, and hippos are apt to be found in or around any freshwater lake.

Sitatunga

The sitatunga is an antelope that lives only in papyrus and reed swamps and flooded forest areas. Virtually aquatic, it has long hoofs that splay widely under its weight, enabling it to walk on sodden vegetation without sinking through. Its oily, shaggy coat is another aquatic adaptation. Where sitatungas occur they tend to be numerous, and individuals have small home ranges.

The sitatunga belongs to the tragelaphine group of slender, deep-bodied antelopes. The male is gray-brown and has keeled horns, each with a spiral one-and-a-half twist. The smaller female is either reddish or gray-brown, and her whitish stripes and spots are more distinct than the male's.

In its watery habitat the sitatunga moves slowly and deliberately along tunnel-like pathways through reeds and papyrus. Tall rushes sway, and hoofs make squelching, sucking sounds. Often the animal is body-deep in water, walking on submerged vegetation. For day bedding, a sitatunga seeks a dry mound or tussock of tall grass. There it circles to trample out a dry, springy bed. On such a nest the female hides her newborn calf for the first weeks of its life.

When surprised by a predator's close approach, a sitatunga bounds off in floundering leaps and splashing water. Usually it detects a predator's coming and remains motionless in dense cover. If the antelope is in water, it submerges slowly until only its nose tip protrudes. Pythons and leopards are its enemies. So are crocodiles, the smaller cats, jackals, and large *raptors* (hawks and eagles). Even lions have been reported to kill sitatunga.

Hippopotamus

At night hippos swim and wade their way into shallow water, creating channels through mats of floating vegetation, and haul themselves ashore. They follow worn tracks to grazing areas that often are considerable distances from water. For several hours they graze, walking slowly and munching loudly, wrenching the short grass with horny lips and a swinging motion of their broad-muzzled heads.

A herd or school, 10 to 100 or more hippos, consists of females, small calves, and juvenile and subadult animals. Bachelor males form groups and live apart, often inland in muddy wallows. Dominant males occupy more choice lake or riverside plots. The basic social unit, however, is the female hippo and her calf.

Hippos and crocodiles often share the same habitat. A basking crocodile either gives way to the hippo and heaves off the sandbar or receives a shove from the mammal's huge head. But a small hippo calf must be protected from crocodiles. It swims close to its mother's side or squats on her broad back. A crocodile's approach elicits a jaw-snap threat from the mother hippo.

Both animals show similar adaptations for their amphibious way of life. Head profiles are similar. Nostrils are set high on the head and can be opened or closed by small encircling muscles. Eyes also are high on the head, for periscopic vision when most of the hippo or croc is underwater. Ears have valvelike closures for swimming below the surface. The hippo's small, rounded ears are set high enough to be swiveled for sounds as it lies immersed.

When it does submerge, a hippo can stay underwater for as long

as four or five minutes. Water is its element. The hippo runs over the bottom on wide, splaying, four-toed feet with the grace of a buoyant ballet dancer or swims, propelled by powerful hind-leg thrusts and movements of its long, supple back. Then it surfaces, expelling water from its nostrils with hissing, and rapidly swiveling its ears to rid them of water. On land, for all its hulk and its short, stumpy legs, a hippo walks briskly and sometimes trots like a warthog.

By morning hippos return to water and doze in placid piles in the shallows. Grooming marks their sociability. They lick, nuzzle, and scrape with their lower incisors. By midday the slow process of digestion is underway and coarsely chewed grass of the night before passes through the three-part stomach and into the intestines. Quantities of manure are discharged into the water, each deposit propelled some distance by rapid whirring of the hippo's vertically compressed short tail. This abundant fertilizer produces a flourishing growth of plankton that sustains fish as well as wading and fishing birds. Dominant male hippos also defecate on rocks and stumps along their inland tracks.

Tail whirring also precedes hippo encounters. Some of these are friendly meetings, others are not. Then mouths snap open with an incredible gape that reveals their brilliant pink interior and an array of dental weaponry. In late afternoon and into the night male hippos contest. Their ritualized mouth-to-mouth combat is accompanied by loud, guttural wheeze-honking. With each clash of lower jaws, one bull tries to snag the other's teeth. Slashing canine tusks often inflict deep gashes. Hippo flanks are marked with granulating scars from such battles.

Dividing time between water, mud wallowing, and sun basking is the hippo's way of thermoregulation. When water is cold, hippos bask. But their thin, purplish gray to blue-black skin loses water by evaporation, so they must return to water or mud for cooling. For this reason, wet season is dispersal time, when hippos travel overland distances in search of new living space.

Colobus Monkey

Surrounding some of the freshwater lakes are luxuriant feverthorn forests. Black-and-white colobus monkeys live among the upper branches, climbing and jumping from tree to tree. In spite of their conspicuous markings, the monkeys are hard to see in the canopy.

Colobus, meaning "mutilated one," was the name given by the first scientists to collect these gentle, leaf-eating monkeys that sometimes became expedition pets. They thought the monkey's thumbs had been cut off. In fact, the colobus's thumbless condition (vestiges of thumbs are visible in the embryonic colobus) facilitates leaping

progression through treetops and brachiating, or swinging by the arms, to land with hands and feet out front. Sometimes when a colobus drops downward it falls with arms and legs outstretched. Then it appears to glide, its long body hairs and flowing white tail functioning as a parachute.

Colobus troops have well-defined home ranges. They remain on one or two feeding trees for a few days, plucking off young leaves and putting them into their mouths by hand. When troops meet, the monkeys jump up and down, white flank fringes waving in agitation, and sound their rattling warning calls.

Within the troop a dominant male is the leader and defender. Babies, born all white, cling to their mother's undersides. At first they receive a one-hand hold when the mother leaps. Then they cling by themselves, small heads against the mother's chest, tiny tails projecting between her hind legs. Young colobus are playful, running off and then jumping their mothers, or pretending to be afraid of a large male. Later on they wrestle and play among themselves.

Crocodile

On land the crocodile is clumsy. Its body arches high over hind legs that are longer and stouter than its forelegs. In spite of its formidable appearance, the crocodile is rather timid. One of the few places to see these big reptiles is along the Nile River just below Kabalega Falls in Uganda. Even here their numbers have been reduced by hunting and poaching.

Small wading birds often are companions of basking crocodiles. Plovers flit over sprawled bodies and run along scaled backs, looking for leeches. When the crocodiles gape to dissipate body heat, the birds sometimes enter their mouths to pick food from their teeth. The "quick-quick-quick" alarm call of the plovers sends the crocodiles slithering on their bellies into the water.

Crocodiles are primarily water animals. Submerging, they glide away with surging thrusts of their huge tails, their limbs folded close to their bodies. To overcome the underwater problem of buoyancy and to prevent rolling over when they loll at the surface, crocodiles ingest pebbles and stones for stomach ballast. They can stay underwater for an hour at a time or longer.

Large fish are a staple in the diet of a crocodile. Now and again birds and mammals are snatched. Crocodile life is leisurely, and a weekly big meal often suffices. Newborn crocodiles—the few that survive to hatching from the 50 or more eggs in the ground nest the female scoops out and tends—feed on aquatic insects. Crocodiles less than a foot long must be wary of a host of predators, including monitor lizards, baboons, mongooses, and marabous. Probably only one in a hundred lives to maturity.

Waterbuck

Swampy grassland valleys and riverine woodlands are grazing areas for herds of waterbuck. These are handsome antelopes, large and heavy-bodied, with oily, shaggy, gray-brown coats and high head carriage. The male has ridged, curved, widely spread, forward-tipped horns. The common waterbuck has a white circle on its rump. The defassa waterbuck has a white rump patch.

Waterbuck are *reduncines,* antelope grazers that live along river edges and lake margins. More aquatic than their reedbuck and kob relatives, they wade in knee- and hock-deep to drink and feed on water plants. Morning and evening are grazing times. By nightfall the herds disperse in small groups, moving into surrounding thicket areas to rest and ruminate.

Social organization includes small herds of 5 to 25 females, young, and subadults, as well as bachelor and spinster groups, temporary associations of young males and young females that may in some instances be outgrowths of nursery herd friendships. Young males spend up to five years in bachelor groups, constantly reinforcing the age-based hierarchy with sparring and horn-grappling contests. While young males are always ready to test their combat skills, older males usually rely on postural displays to avoid fighting.

Waterbuck are sedentary by nature. When an adult male establishes his own territory, he becomes more attached to his land than to others of his species. The female, too, tends to become attached to an area as she grows older, moving about within a home range that overlaps the territories of several males.

Young hoofed mammals are cared for in two basic ways. Some are followers, on their feet soon after birth to move with the herd. Others, like waterbuck calves, are hiders in tall grass or thicket. Two or three times a day the mother comes to her calf. Only after she has nudged and licked its thin neck does the calf respond and get up to suckle. Then, left behind when the cow bounds away, the calf lies down to hide again until her return. This period of hiding allows time for the calf to develop and gain coordination for avoiding predators. Even more importantly, it is an isolation period during which *imprinting,* mutual recognition between cow and calf, takes place. By the fourth week, when calf and cow join with other females and their young, there is time for play. Calves charge about and chase each other. Sometimes warthogs are their playmates.

Waterbuck, especially calves, are frequently killed by hyenas, lions, and leopard. Crocodiles occasionally snatch adults that wade into water to drink. Cheetahs also prey on calves. Usually a waterbuck's defense is to flee and then hide motionless in bush or tall grass. To elude a pursuing pack of hyenas or wild dogs, a waterbuck bounds into the water and submerges.

Reedbuck

Small, reddish fawn antelopes with white belly and white eye rings and a conspicuous round patch of bare skin below each ear, reedbucks live in pairs or loosely formed groups, always near water.

Female reedbucks (up to five) have overlapping home ranges within a male's territory. In a sense the females are the male's territory, for he jealously guards them, rather than an area of ground. He is intolerant of young males. As soon as their spike horns develop, he drives them off to seek living space in between the territories of adult males.

Seasonal flushes of good grazing cause concentrations of reedbucks. Sometimes they join with topi, kob, and other grazers. Early morning and dusk are grazing times; during the day they lie hidden in reeds or make formlike shelters in deep grass.

Alarm is signaled by a shrill whistle. Usually crouching is the first reaction. Then, at the last moment, the reedbucks break cover and gallop off in rocking-horse bounds, legs rigid and tails flagging white.

Crowned Crane

An elegant, tall bird with black velvety forehead and a crown of bristly straw-colored feathers frequents marshes and wet grassland areas. On the ground the crowned crane is stately and storklike. A distinguishing crane feature is its short hind toe, markedly elevated above the three front toes and supporting none of the bird's weight as it strides along.

Cranes stamp through the grass, scaring insects to flight, and seizing them as they rise. They also eat worms, snails, lizards and snakes, and occasionally small birds and mammals. In soft ground they probe and dig for roots and grubs. And they forage for grains.

Cranes fly like geese, with necks extended and gooselike honking. When they visit a water hole or lake they drink by plunging their long bill almost nostril deep, then raising the head for a quick swallow.

5 The Bush

The *nyika,* or East African bushland, is a vast area of thorny thickets in eastern Kenya and Tanzania. Hot and waterless for much of the year, the bush is a place where rainfall is scant. Plants compete for what moisture there is and are adapted in various ways for conserving it. Some have deep root systems for tapping water. Others have bulbs and tubers for underground water storage or swollen stems or waxy, succulent leaves for aboveground storage. Except for the huge-boled gray baobab, or upside-down tree, that looks as though its roots and not its branches were above ground, few trees grow large in the bush. During the long dry season, when near-desert conditions prevail, the landscape is colored gray and ochre, and much of the leafless vegetation appears dead.

The rains, when they come, cause rivers to rise and dried-up *dongas* (stream beds) to flashflood. Suddenly there is a flush of green leaves and flowers, but only for a short time.

Mammals, too, are adapted for bush life. Many of the larger ones are wanderers, traveling long distances for water. Others can do without drinking. Most of them are browsers. Within the same habitat they avoid direct competition by ecological separation that is vertical as well as horizontal. Some animals prefer rocky hillsides and gullies; others are found on flat terrain. Tall browsers, especially the giraffe, browse high up, sometimes on tops of trees. Dik-diks take only twigs and leaves of the lowest branches. Most of the hoofed

mammals have slender muzzles for browsing among thorns and spines. The giraffe's long, prehensile tongue and the black rhino's hooked upper lip are browsing adaptations. So is the elephant's trunk.

"In the high and Far-Off Times the Elephant . . . had no trunk. He had only a blackish, bulgy nose." According to Rudyard Kipling, it was a crocodile that pulled the nose of a little elephant, "full of satiable curtiosity, . . . into a really truly trunk same as all Elephants have to-day."

This happened along the banks of the "great grey-green, greasy Limpopo River, all set about with fever-trees," where the little elephant met a crocodile and asked "Will you please tell me what you have for dinner?" "Come hither . . . and I'll whisper," replied the crocodile. The elephant leaned down close to the crocodile's "musky, tusky mouth, and the Crocodile caught him by his little nose." Sitting back on his small haunches the elephant pulled and pulled and as he pulled his nose "stretched and kept on stretching."★

*Excerpted from "The Elephant's Child." Rudyard Kipling, *Just So Stories* (New York, Doubleday and Co, 1907), pp. 65–67, 70–72.

African Elephant

The elephant's trunk is both sensory organ and food-gathering tool. Actually it is a heavily muscled *proboscis,* the outgrowth of the elephant's nose and upper lip. It can be twisted or coiled to pick up food or extended for siphoning water from stream bed or water hole. Assisted by the scuff of a forefoot, it can be used to break roots. In wrestling bouts the trunk is a powerful weapon. It also is capable of delicate movements—picking fruits from a tree or off the ground, rubbing an eye, or comforting a calf.

In spite of its great size and enormous body weight, the elephant

is a very mobile animal. To support its bulk it has columnar legs. Its toes, contained within an almost circular foot of skin and nails, are supported by an elastic pad. Ambling, so that each hind foot moves into the print left by the forefoot of the same side, the elephant strides through forest, bush, savanna, or across the open grassland.

Whatever their habitat, elephants have impact on their environment, stripping and eating bark, smashing bushes, and knocking down trees.

Forest elephants, like forest forms of other large animals, are smaller than savanna elephants. They tend to have longer legs and have slender tusks. Their habits are not seasonal, for climate is fairly constant in the forest, and food is always available. Forest elephants move in circuits within their home range, occasionally appearing in open areas.

Tusks, enlarged upper incisor teeth, are used for fighting. Young males spar. Between big bulls, competing for an *estrous* cow, contests

are real. Females use their tusks to disperse young males that annoy their family group. Tusks are often broken. In fact, tuskless males are reputed to be bullies, relying on displays of aggression and bluff, butting and ear-flapping.

Molar teeth, six on each side of upper and lower jaws, succeed one another during an elephant's life: first three milk molars, then three permanent molars in succession. As one molar is worn down by grinding, another moves forward in the jaw to replace it. These huge teeth and their sequence and wear make it possible to estimate an elephant's age. An aged elephant eventually has no teeth. Unable to chew food, it dies of starvation.

Elephant relationships are many-tiered. First there is a cow and her infant calf. The bond between them is a strong one. Surrounding this

nucleus is the cow's family group, her older calves. These siblings fondle the small calf and act as baby-sitters. An elephant calf, born after a long, 21- to 22-month gestation, grows slowly and needs care. Beyond the family group is the cow's bond group, composed of three

or four other family groups. The cow is on friendly terms and in frequent contact with all these elephants. Bond groups in turn form clans of eight or nine family groups. Still larger assemblages (about 30 groups) form a subpopulation. Finally there is the entire elephant population of an area, perhaps some 50 groups whose cow-calf units number over 400 elephants and include 100 or more adult bulls.

Scent is the elephant's most highly developed sense. Jonathan Kingdon describes coming upon a family group making their way,

single-file up a woodland path. He moved off the path and downwind to let the elephants pass. ". . . at the point where I had halted, the matriarch leader made a slight scooping motion with the tip of her trunk in the dust and immediately turned to follow my most recent footsteps with pointed trunk held close to the ground. . . . she gave

a wheezing squeal and flapped her ears but it was clear that she could neither see or hear me and was displaying purely on the evidence of the fresh scent left at my passage or by my shoes."[*]

Bulls are often solitary. Sometimes they associate in small herds, but these are temporary associations. The sparring of young bulls in these herds establishes an order of rank. In later life it will be enough for these same bulls to communicate by postural signals when they meet and thus avoid actual combat.

Environmental conditions influence elephant groupings, and regional and seasonal differences are apparent. During the dry season, browsing is better done in small groups—a cow by herself, or with her young calf, or in a small bond or clan group. The rains bring a rapid fresh growth of vegetation, and elephants tend to move in large aggregations into good browsing areas.

---

[*]Jonathan Kingdon, *East African Mammals,* Vol. IIIB (New York, Academic Press, 1979), p. 62.

Home range size is correlated with habitat. In lush habitats an elephant's home range may be no more than 15 square kilometers (9.4 square miles), while in very arid regions individuals range over more than 3,000 square kilometers (1,863 square miles). All kinds of vegetation are food for elephants. Their feeding does relatively little damage during the rainy season when grass is abundant. As dry conditions return, grass tussocks are ripped from the ground by their trunks and swished against their shoulders to get rid of soil that clings to the moisture-containing roots. Soon the large herds disperse, and elephants resume their rough browsing techniques of breaking trees and stripping bark. They travel long distances for water. Severe drought finds them in stream beds, using their trunks to excavate water holes.

Much of an elephant herd's day is spent eating. Rumbling, growling contact calls keep the browsing group together in the bush. Alarm causes them to cluster around the oldest cow, or matriarch, to confront the danger or wait until she decides the direction in which the herd will flee.

A wounded or dying elephant is the object of group concern. It is nudged and prodded in attempt to get it up. There have been incidences of two elephants, one on either side, actually moving off with a wounded elephant pressed between, supported by their hulking bodies. Sometimes a cow elephant stands solitary vigil over her dead calf for days before finally rejoining her group. Such accounts have made this huge animal with its trunk and loose, wrinkled skin a legend among the animals of Africa.

Dik-dik

A persistent whistling call gives this dwarf antelope its name. Adapted for life in arid low-thicket habitats, the dik-dik has internal methods of conserving water. It gets its water from its browse. Kidneys concentrate urine, and sweat glands produce very little moisture. Even the dik-dik's most conspicuous feature, a flexible Roman nose, or proboscis, is a cooling device, providing increased evaporative surface.

Activity patterns also reflect the dik-diks' need to conserve water. They browse from dusk to midnight, plucking leaves with tongue and upper lip. Then, lying in a thicket or near the trunk of a tree, with their small legs folded neatly beneath their bodies, they rest and ruminate. At dawn they feed again. Midday heat is avoided by a long period of rest and rumination. Always they are alert, relying on their eyes, well set for wide-angle vision, to detect predators.

Dik-diks live in pairs. Both male and female are familiar with the one- to five-hectare (two-and-a-half- to twelve-acre) territory they occupy. When surprised by a predator, dik-diks crouch, head extended on the ground and eyes closed. More often the predator is sighted at a distance. Then the dik-diks whistle and race for cover, *pronking* or *stotting* in stiff-legged, bouncing leaps, whistling each time their tiny hoofs strike the ground. Often they circle within their home range.

Racing for cover expends energy and causes a rapid increase in breathing rate and rise in body temperature. The dik-dik pants heavily. As it pants, dry air flows over the moist lining of its bellowslike nasal chambers. Evaporation occurs and causes cooling of the blood in the vessels that supply the nasal lining. As venous blood it drains back to pool around a network of capillaries that interrupts the flow of arterial blood to the brain. The heat exchange that occurs between venous and arterial blood prevents fatal overheating of the brain.

Dik-dik territories are marked by dung piles along their perimeters, which are relocated from time to time. While a neighboring dik-dik's manure causes little concern, an interloper's dung deposit is sniffed, scratched, and deposited upon by the resident dik-dik. Attempts are also made to obliterate the dung of other, larger antelopes. Dik-diks even drop their pellets on rhino manure and elephant balls. Jonathan Kingdon relates an African folktale about the "territorial pretensions" of this diminutive antelope.

"A dik-dik one day stumbled over a ball of elephant dung and was so cross that he then always used the same place in the hope that one day it would be sufficiently large to trip up the elephant."★

Two males contest a boundary with high-stepping. Heads are held high and crests fanned out. They make false jabs at each other with their small horns. All of this is ritual behavior that usually precludes a serious fight.

A dik-dik pair is a family unit. The female is pregnant much of the time, mating occurring about ten days after each birth. Both dik-diks share parental duties. Their fawn is hidden for the first weeks. Even in infancy the fawn's crouch-and-freeze response is well developed and exhibited each time its parents approach to nuzzle, suckle, and groom their offspring.

★Jonathan Kingdon, *East African Mammals,* Vol. IIIC (New York, Academic Press, 1982), p. 257

Secretary Bird

Striding on storklike long legs through dry, short grass, heads nodding and quill-pen feathers ruffled by the wind, a pair of secretary birds hunt. Now and again the measured stalking strides of these three-and-a-half-foot-tall terrestrial hawks give way to zigzag running and wing flapping, and stamping when a rodent or grasshopper is caught.

The male strikes a snake, stamping rapidly with both legs to kill it. With hooked beak he will tear the snake into pieces for swallowing.

Dusk will find the birds in the thorn tree where their large stick nest is located. They roost until well after sunrise, waiting for warmth before they jump to the ground to begin another day's foraging.

Black Rhinoceros

An inhabitant of bush country, the black rhino browses on coarse, prickly vegetation. Adult males lead solitary lives, but a female, usually with a calf (newborn to three years old) at her side, often has the company of another female. In the eyes of Isak Dinesen, two rhinos "on their morning promenade . . . looked like two very big angular stones rollicking in the long valley and enjoying life together."*

---

*Out of Africa, p. 15

Home ranges overlap and vary in size according to availability of browse and seasonal conditions. Rhinos are scent-oriented. They rely on dung deposits, which they scrape with their hind feet. The males urine-spray to assert their presence. These signposts are used to follow up or to avoid social and sexual contacts.

Within its home range a rhino lives with routine. Early morning is for browsing as the rhino moves along well-known paths or tunnels through thorn thickets, the brush scraping against its armored sides. Midday is for resting. Rhinos doze standing or lying down in shade, or more often lie in full sun in a dust-filled wallow. Chin or cheek to the ground, the resting rhino lies on its brisket, legs curled beneath its huge body, its ears constantly swiveling.

Red-billed oxpeckers, or tickbirds, cling to rhinos' cracked hides, looking for parasites and working at blood-encrusted sores caused by a threadlike parasitic worm transmitted by flies and ticks. When the birds fly up, wheeling and shrieking, rhinos become alert.

Cattle egrets (or buff-backed herons) are also sentinels. Perched on a rhino's back or feeding on insects stirred up by its feet, the birds fly up in alarm when a predator appears.

With a sharp, puffing snort the rhino is on its feet. It stands blinking, swinging its head from side to side. Head raised and ears forward, it takes a few nervous steps. If two rhinos are together, they stand with rumps touching and facing in different directions. Then, heads high, they move off through thick grass or bush. If the predator is located, the rhino charges, head lowered, puffing and snorting, tail up, and moving with locomotive speed.

Mud wallowing, a favorite afternoon pastime, is a way of cooling off and getting rid of ticks. The rhino goes down first on one side, then sits up, rotates on its hindquarters, and drops for a roll on the other side. The length of its vertebral spines prohibits rolling over. A coating of mud not only conditions the hide but gives some protection from biting flies. As it flakes off, a scent trail is left for other rhinos.

Wallowing makes rhinos the color of their habitat. Black rhinos are gray. In Amboseli National Park, where soils are alkaline, rhinos are whitish gray. In the Tsavo parks rhinos have reddish hides that are nearly the color of the Tsavo soil. Except for a few here-and-there hairs that protrude, a rhino is naked. Its only hairs are eyelashes, ear fringes, and tail-tip bristles.

Early evening is another time of intensive feeding. The black rhino is a selective browser, sniffing as it moves from bush to bush. Its pointed, prehensile upper lip wraps around twigs and leaves and draws them into the mouth to be chewed or snapped off by premolar teeth. Sometimes, to reach succulent leaves high up on a thorn tree, the rhino rears up.

Water holes are nighttime meeting places where rhinos are markedly tolerant of each other. Meeting often involves puffing snorts, sometimes a rubbing of cheeks, or a jousting with horns. When two bulls meet, mutual displays often develop into sparring matches. Like hockey players the two rhinos clash.

Nearsightedness and a tendency to rush forward, puffing and snorting, when danger is scented account for the black rhino's reputation as a bad-tempered animal. A rhino, according to Norman Myers, "charges with great thoroughness and speed: sometimes because it catches a movement in the bushes, sometimes because it gets a whiff of something strange, sometimes just because it is a rhino."★

Studying rhinos in Ngorongoro Crater and in Tsavo National Park, John Goddard developed a special feeling for these massive beasts he found to have individual "temperaments, moods, and, to be quite unscientific, personality."

Rhinos consort in pairs for about four months during breeding season. After an 18-month gestation, the calf is born. Vulnerable to predation by hyenas and lions, it stays close beside its mother. Its horn is a small, round nasal nubbin.

★Norman Myers, *The Long African Day* (New York, Macmillan, 1972), p. 187.

Rhino horns, unlike those of bovids (antelopes and cattle), are not sheaths that cover central bone cores on the skull. Composed of fibrous, hairlike material, they are attached to thick skin and are easily removed from the rhino, a fact that has cost many rhinos their lives. Trade in rhino horns for medicinal uses has gone on for centuries in the Far East. In recent years poaching has increased to alarming proportions. Demand for rhino horns has burgeoned in Yemen, where Saudi Arabian oil has produced sudden wealth and men wear *jambias,* or daggers with handles of carved rhino horn, as symbols of their manhood. Efforts are being made to stop poaching and, more importantly, to put an end to the demand for rhino horns.

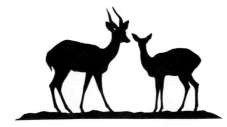

Bushbuck

Identified by a rump that is higher than its shoulders, the bushbuck is deerlike in outline. The male's short horns form only the first loop of a spiral.

Marginal habitats between grassland and forest are the favorite haunts. Montane forests, riverine forests, and dense bushland also are home to these shy, elusive antelopes. According to where they live, bushbuck vary in color from bright chestnut red, with a conspicuous harness of white stripes and spots, to brown with almost no markings.

Wherever they live, bushbuck slip quietly in and out of thickets. Large ears suggest that sound, for these bush dwellers, is more important than sight. During the day bushbuck rest in thick cover. At night they browse on leaves, shoots, acacia pods, tubers, and roots, and crop some grass.

Lesser Kudu

A lesser kudu calf remains in its hiding place for a month or so after birth. Its typical tragelaphine coloration is camouflage during the hiding period. To gain attention or to suckle, the calf makes use of the lateral display, halting broadside in front of its mother. By the time it is two or three months old, the calf accompanies its mother on short browsing excursions, and soon they join a herd with other cows and calves.

Smaller size and brownish or bluish gray color (that merges with dry season twigs and branches when the antelope freezes) distinguish the lesser kudu from its larger relative. Eleven to 15 vertical white stripes mark its slender body. Instead of a fringe of throat hairs such as the greater kudu has, there are two white throat patches, markings that are conspicuous in head-up displays among lesser kudus.

Although it is more like the greater kudu in appearance, the lesser kudu is more like another tragelaphine relative, the bushbuck, in its habits. Sharing the same scrub-thicket and semiarid bush habitats, the lesser kudu's ability to go longer without drinking and reach higher for browse makes for little overlap in the ranges of the two species.

Gerenuk

Rising on her hind legs, two meters tall against a honey-scented acacia, a gerenuk sniffs about with her delicately pointed muzzle. With mobile lips and long, slender tongue she selects and plucks a leaf at a time. An upward jerk of her head gives a cutting action to her spoon-shaped lower incisor teeth.

A gerenuk is the ultimate browser, standing tall on its thin hind legs, its body perfectly balanced. To support this unusual way of feeding, it has carried the *gazelline* antelope trend of lengthened limbs and neck to the extreme. Metatarsals (long bones, from hock or ankle to fetlock joint) are elongated and strong. The spines of the lower back vertebrae are modified for attachment of powerful back muscles used in standing upright. Through time this antelope's neck vertebrae (the usual seven in number found in all mammals) have lengthened,

and superficial neck muscles have been reduced, giving the gerenuk a long, slender neck, useful in reaching high browse. *Gerenuk* is a Somali word meaning "giraffe-necked."

Gerenuks have a horizontal three-toned pattern of russet, light chestnut, and white. When they stand erect, their white undersides are conspicuous.

In their arid bush habitat gerenuks feed selectively from a wide variety of plants at different stages of growth. Their dry-season diet includes evergreen plants that few other browsers will touch. Sometimes they browse on wilted leaves and dry, brittle twigs. Thickets are avoided. Gerenuks prefer to browse around the perimeters or over the tops of clumps of bushes. Dawn and dusk are times of active feeding. During the day the gazelles stand resting or lie down in the shade. There are no water holes and few rivers that flow where gerenuks live.

Adult males maintain territories that are both for feeding and for breeding. In arid parts of Kenya's Tsavo National Park three to six square kilometers (1.8 to 3.7 square miles) is the size of a male's territory. Within this area he may be seen alone. More often he is in the company of several females whose home ranges are within his territory. He is proprietary about both his land and his females, marking twigs and gerenuks with secretion from his preorbital gland. This staking of property insures adequate browse for the small group of females and their offspring, as well as his own breeding rights.

Free-ranging younger males are always ready to usurp a land holding. The head nodding and head rubbing used in gerenuk greetings and among females to establish rank gives way to heads-low horn clashing. The males' lyre-shaped, heavily ringed horns are supported by bony reinforcement of their skulls.

For the first weeks of life, a gerenuk fawn is concealed under a bush. Its birth coincides with the greening that comes after rains. Its mother browses with the other gerenuks, making brief visits to touch noses and suckle her infant. By its fifth week the fawn follows its mother and moves with the gerenuk group.

When alarmed, gerenuks usually freeze. Standing (or sometimes lying down) motionless, they stare over or around bushes and trees. Then, females first and male behind, they move off at a fluid trot, necks and tails carried horizontally, or bound off at a gallop, pronking as though on springs or darting under and around bushes to escape

the predator's rush. For gerenuk and other bush-dwelling antelopes, leaping and the ability to maneuver are more important than speed and endurance.

Elephant Shrew

Belonging to a family (the Macroscelididae) found only in Africa and having no close relatives among other living mammals is the elephant shrew. This rat-sized *insectivore* has an elongated, mobile, trunklike snout, hind legs that are longer than its forelegs, and a long tail.

Except where harassed by predators or when it is very hot, the elephant shrew is active during the day. Ants and termites, grasshoppers, and beetles make up much of its diet. Small pathways, irregularly worn by the elephant shrew's bouncing leaps, extend out from its shelter in a rock pile, hollow log, or among the roots of a tree, to feeding places. In its bushland habitat, usually three or four families live in close proximity. Where spiny mice are numerous, elephant shrews tend to be absent.

Gestation is long for so small a mammal, about 50 days. The one or two young have a miniature-adult appearance that correlates with a lifestyle of aboveground activity without the safety of a secure nest. When a raptor soars overhead, a young elephant shrew responds to its mother's alarm signal, a rapid hind-foot tapping, and dashes for safety under a shrub.

Greater Kudu

Rocky hill and mountain terrain, with dense bush cover and flat bushland where there are water holes, are habitats for greater kudus. Where they graze, the bateleur eagle also soars in search of a meal. Spotting a snake, it descends with a quick, fanning action of its white-lined wings. The bateleur is a striking raptor with chestnut back,

black body, and red legs. In spite of having long, narrow wings and a very short tail, it is an efficient glider. Once the air has warmed, the bateleur lifts off to begin its daylong, low-altitude soaring search for small animal prey.

Herds of six to twenty greater kudus, mostly females and young, are joined briefly by dominant males during breeding season. At other times bulls live singly or in bachelor groups.

When frightened, a kudu freezes. The six to ten vertical white stripes on its sandy, yellowish sides simulate sunlight streaking through concealing gray twigs and branches. Then, in panic, the kudu takes off with huge leaps, tail turned up over its back to reveal the bushy white underside.

Both sexes are tall, long necked and long legged, and have a spinal crest. Occasionally a female has horns. The male has huge spiral horns that, in combination with his powerful maned neck and hair-tasseled *dewlap* emphasize his forequarters. Horns are almost never used on enemies. Instead they are shields, used as males contest each other, horn wrestling and pushing spiral curve against spiral curve. Even this form of horned combat is infrequent. More often, rank among males is established by lateral displays. The males slowly circle one another with spinal crests erect and high-stepping gait.

As in all tragelaphine society, male hierarchy is based on age. The older a bull, the more impressive is his appearance. With age body color darkens, and contrasting markings become more conspicuous.

Kudu calves are born during the rainy season when there is moist grass for the cows. Except for suckling visits from the mother, the calf lies hidden for the first month. Then it moves with its mother more and more and soon finds other calves in the herd for playmates.

Oryx

Lengthened vertebral spines and a well-developed nuchal (neck) ligament, as well as a compact, barrel-shaped body contribute to the oryx's high-shouldered, deep-chested, horselike outline. This *hippotragine* (an antelope group that includes roan and sable) has large hoofs adapted for sure-footed, long-striding travel over rough ground.

Striking black-on-white facial markings and black on forelegs and tail contrast with grayish-fawn body color. A forehead patch that connects with a wide nasal stripe and a dark line on either side of the head accentuates the long line of its nearly straight, ringed horns. A facial stripe, connecting under the throat and running down the underside of the neck, also emphasizes head gestures. In lateral display postures the horizontal slash of black, separating fawn body from white belly, stands out.

Mixed herds of 20 or more oryxes usually have a dominant male and sometimes another male of rank. Females have their own hierarchy based on age or length of herd association. Other males, juveniles, and young calves make up the rest of the herd. Even would-be herd joiners are tolerated.

The herd moves in single file, then spreads out to graze. When predators appear the antelopes usually gallop off. Occasionally an oryx leaves the herd to turn and face a pack of hyenas or wild dogs, rushing at the pursuers and making circular sweeps with its horns.

A sudden wind or rain shower sometimes causes one or more individuals, often young animals, to gallop in circles about the rest of the herd. Abruptly the gallop drops off to a hackneyed trot with slow, elevated leg movements. The head is high and carried well back on the neck so that facial stripes and horns form a nearly horizontal line. With each exaggerated, knee-snapping stride, the oryx swings its head, flashing its black markings as well as those of forelegs and hoofs. Clash-provoking head feints are made at herd members. If a challenge is accepted a match ensues, a collision of horns that is a ritualized testing of rank within the herd.

Aggression between two bulls is marked by the same posture. Circling each other at a measured walk, opponents paw, then clash. They parry blows with their horns as each bull attempts to knock the other off balance rather than to skewer him.

Oryxes are wanderers of dry rocky desert areas in northern Kenya (the beisa oryx) and scrub-thicket habitats of southern Kenya and northern Tanzania (the fringe-eared oryx). The ultimate desert dwellers are the gemsbok of southern Africa's Kalahari Desert and the Arabian and scimitar-horned oryxes of northern Africa.

Although they do come to drink where water is available, oryxes are among the hoofed mammals that can go for long periods without water. Physiologist C. Richard Taylor found that an oryx deprived of water pants when its body temperature rises above 41°C, while an oryx with water available sweats. This is one of this antelope's strategies for preventing water loss in an arid habitat. There are others. When oryxes stand out in the heat of midday, making no effort to find shade, their light-colored coats reflect some heat (desert oryxes are lightest in color). Metabolism slows during the day to reduce the heat burden. Stored heat is dissipated by cooler night temperatures. And by feeding mostly at night, oryxes get some moisture from condensation on dry, brittle grasses and shrub-browse. During drought oryxes dig with their front hoofs for roots and tubers. In some places they make seasonal moves in search of better grazing.

6 Savannas

Spreading west and east across the breadth of Africa, savanna land-scapes are intermediate between open grasslands and forests. Widely scattered umbrella-shaped thorn trees towering above a sea of grass are characteristic of climatic (climate-influenced) savannas, produced by rainfall concentrated in part of the year, followed by a long period of drought. There are also edaphic (soil-influenced) savannas, developed on hills and ridges where volcanic soil is shallow or in valleys where clay soil becomes waterlogged when it rains, then cracks deeply as it dries out.

Fire is an important factor in savanna maintenance. Sometimes it is caused by lightning; often it is set by herdsmen to improve grazing for their livestock. In the fire's wake, tender shoots sprout from roots of burned grasses and shrubs. Grazing and trampling also affect and extend savanna areas.

The *miombo* woodlands stretch from southern Tanzania and Mozambique to southern Zaire and Angola. Deep, sandy soils support a monotonous sparse covering of trees that in some areas are tall growing, in others gnarled and scrublike, but always of uniform height. Beneath the scattered trees tall grass grows.

These woodlands alternate with wide, flat grassy valleys *(mbugas)*, flooded during the wet season but utilized by zebras, waterbuck, sable and roan antelopes, and hartebeests in the dry season, when woodland grasses have dried out.

Sable Antelope

The sable has scythelike horns, a long face and ears, a short neck, and a compact, well-rounded body. Its color depends upon age and status within the herd. A mature bull is blue-black with contrasting white facial markings and a white belly. He stands out in the herd, his arched neck and horselike stance proclaiming his dominance. In fact, by such dominance displays he asserts his territory. Dung piles also define his territory. Patrolling at night as well as during the day, he climbs on termite mounds, uses his ridged horns to scrape bark and mark trees, occasionally drops to his knees and horns the ground, and paws with his front hoofs. If a challenger persists, a vigorous fight ensues.

Within their wooded habitat, sables move about seasonally in search of good grass and water, a daily necessity for these antelopes. Rainy season finds sables dispersed in small herds. When woodland grasses dry out, sable herds gather and migrate in search of green grass, often feeding on leaves as well.

In the Shimba Hills near the Kenya coast, where there is water year-round, sable herds stay put within the 13-square-kilometer (8-square-mile) area. Here Richard D. Estes mapped the overlapping ranges of some five herds and found that they extended over a number of male territories.

The sable bull takes control over any herd that moves onto his territory. He approaches each of the cows, testing for ones in estrus. When they stray toward the boundary, he snorts and gestures with his horns to keep them within his one- to four-square-mile territory.

Herds consist of cows and young. The territorial bull, when present, is dominant. Within the herd cows have their own hierarchy, established by fighting. Older females, nearly as dark as the bull, have highest rank. Their head carriage is high, and they tilt and jab with their horns. Their hostility to females outside the group keeps sable herds well spaced. The oldest female is the herd leader.

Calving coincides with the end of the rains. The calf is dun colored and has no facial markings. For several weeks it remains concealed in the grass, visited at nighttime intervals for suckling by its mother. When they join the herd, calves stay together at the rear of the group except when they seek out their mothers to nurse.

At the end of their second year young males are driven from the herd by the bull. They live for several years in bachelor groups of one to eleven other young males. Frequent mock battles are waged in bachelor herds. When the young bulls are five to six years old, their russet-red coats begin to turn shiny blue-black. Soon they are ready to assume their roles as territory holders.

Fights between mature bulls are marked by circling, pawing, and tail lashing. Shaking their heads, the two bulls drop onto their knees. Horns lock. They shove, then jab, horn against horn. On their territories bulls are vulnerable. Not only are they attached to a relatively small area, but they are preoccupied with its defense. If frightened, sables gallop off a short distance, then halt and look back. Trophy hunters as well as predators take advantage of this behavior.

In the ever-increasing competition for habitat, grass, and water, sables and other hoofed animals are protected to some degree by the tsetse flies that are prevalent throughout the miombo and other wooded savanna areas. Tsetses carry one-celled blood parasites called *trypanosomes* that cause various kinds of sleeping sickness in human beings and domestic animals. Wild animals are resistent to tsetse-transmitted diseases. These blood-sucking flies thus limit the spread of human settlement, the extent of grazing, and the monopoly of water holes by herders with their hump-backed zebu and long-horned Ankole cattle.

Roan Antelope

Most horselike of all the hippotragine antelopes is the reddish-gray roan, found in parts of northern Uganda, Tanzania, and in the Shimba Hills. Zebras and elands are often the roan's grazing companions. Roans prefer more open grassland than do sables. Where their grazing areas overlap, competition is reduced by the two antelopes' different feeding habits. Roans prefer medium- to short-length grasses, while sables select taller grasses. For daytime resting they move into the shade of a cluster of trees or shrubs or into the forest margin.

Herds of four to fifteen females, their calves, and a bull form closely knit associations. Although one herd bull may be replaced by another, the females maintain their hierarchy for at least several years. In the herd the calves play-fight and begin to establish ranking order. Juvenile bulls form bachelor groups and skirmish among themselves.

The roan antelope's contrasting black-and-white facial markings, its black ear tufts, and its dark tail heighten signals used in communication. Unlike the sable bull, the roan bull is not territorial. In the herd, his behavior is much like that of a high-ranking cow, but he is readily identified by his massive neck, head, and horns. Horn grapplings and jousting between roan bulls, however, are bloodier than sable bull contests.

Giraffe

"I had time after time watched the progression across the plain of the Giraffe, in their queer, inimitable, vegetative gracefulness, as if it were not a herd of animals but a family of rare, long-stemmed, speckled gigantic flowers slowly advancing."*

Height, body size, and grace are characteristic of these tallest of mammals. Long legs for ambling and galloping and a long neck and periscopic vision for seeing long distances are adaptations for savanna life. So is body size. The giraffe's size is a deterrent to predators. It is also a passive solar mechanism, allowing heat to build up gradually during the day (raising body temperature 3° to 10° C). Since the giraffe neither sweats nor pants, body heat is stored, to be dissipated at night when air temperatures are cooler.

The several geographic races of giraffes differ according to shade and shape of their markings. The reticulated giraffe of northeastern Africa has a reticulate, or netlike, pattern of white that forms large geometric patches on its dark chestnut hide. Baringo, or Rothschild's, giraffes, of Uganda, southern Sudan, and parts of Kenya have wider

*Isak Dinesen, *Out of Africa,* p. 15.

buff-white lines and a lighter-colored blotched pattern. Masai giraffes of Kenya and Tanzania have jagged or leafy chestnut-brown spots on a yellowish buff background. Giraffes of southern Africa have blotched and starlike spot patterns and legs that are spotted below knees and hocks.

While bulls tend to be transients and wander more widely than females, home ranges are restricted—except during the wet season—by the giraffes' dependence on water. They browse in open woodlands and wooded grasslands, usually where there are scattered acacia trees. Hairy lips and long, muscular tongues gather foliage above 2.2 meters (7 feet) and below 5.5 meters (18 feet), a browsing height antelopes cannot reach.

Giraffes feed selectively, shredding off leaves with their rough tongues and nipping off branch tips with their sharp incisors. They browse for 16 to 20 hours a day, pruning trees into hourglass and globular shapes and trimming shrub heights. Then they move off to rest and ruminate. As the partly fermented fodder passes from the rumen (the first part of the four-part ruminant stomach) into the reticulum, cuds, or boluses, are formed. One bolus at a time is regurgitated and forced visibly up the long, muscular esophagus. It is rechewed with a slow, rotatory motion of the lower jaw until it is reduced to pulp, and then swallowed again for digestive passage through the third and fourth parts of the stomach.

Giraffes, like okapi and gerenuk, pace. The long legs on one side of the body move forward at nearly the same time, an adaptation that prevents interference (hitting of forefoot by hind foot) in long-legged mammals. As stride lengthens, speed increases. To prevent toppling, the giraffe's long neck functions as a counterbalance.

The giraffe's other gait is a gallop. Hindquarter muscles bunch as hind legs flare wide to reach forward outside the forelegs. With each propulsive stride, head and neck swing forward and then back. The tail is carried up, its whisk of black hairs streaming in the wind.

Long necks also serve bulls in necking, or head-slamming contests. Stiff-legged, with muzzles in the air, the bulls approach. They circle, then stand shoulder to shoulder. Legs are splayed for balance, as necks are swung out and back to deliver hammerlike blows of bone-reinforced skulls. Necking is the way male giraffes establish a dominance hierarchy and avoid serious fights.

A newborn calf receives close attention from its mother. She will not tolerate the approach of another giraffe. Nudging, nuzzling, licking, and suckling are important in formation of the cow-calf bond. A few weeks later, the mother leaves her calf in a nursery group, or crèche, while she goes off to browse for most of the day. The calves stand about, nibble leaves, play, or lie down in a cluster, facing in different directions. An "auntie," an adult female giraffe, always has a watchful eye on the calves. Because of their relatively small body

size, young giraffes are unable to tolerate midday heat in the open. Their need for shade means a prolonged period of hiding.

By its fifth month the calf accompanies its mother on short browsing forays. A month later it moves and feeds with the other giraffes.

Lions, hyenas, and leopards kill young giraffes. Calf mortality is high (50 to 73 percent) during the first year. Defending her calf with powerful foreleg strikes, a mother giraffe sometimes lands a blow that injures or kills a predator.

A resting giraffe stands or lies down with legs folded beneath its body. For short periods it sleeps, head resting on rump or hind leg, but most of the time it is alert, head up.

Spiny Mouse

The spiny mouse is a *nocturnal* rodent of dry savanna and woodland habitats. It is gray-brown with a white belly and has a protective cape of spiny hairs over its back. It makes its home in a *termitary* (a fortress of baked earth cemented over many seasons with termite saliva and excrement), a rock crevice, or an abandoned burrow. It feeds on seeds, leaves, and occasional insects.

Spiny mice are highly social. The birth of a litter is attended by other females acting as midwives, biting through the umbilical cord of each newborn mouse.

Eland

Largest of the antelopes, elands are nomadic browsers that are sometimes grazers. They can be seen almost anywhere, for their extensive range includes the savanna and grass-woodland zones that cover much of central and southern Africa. There are two kinds of elands. The grayish-fawn common eland prefers open savanna and is found from Ethiopia and southern Zaire to South Africa. The giant eland, over five feet at the shoulder, is reddish-fawn colored, has a larger dewlap, and longer, more massive horns. It lives in a woodland belt that stretches from Senegal east into southern Sudan.

Elands are opportunistic feeders. Their diet varies with the seasons. During the wet season they are plains grazers. When dry season comes they move into bush areas where there is permanent browse. Often they use horns or hoofs to break off branches for nibbling.

Bulls are seen singly or in small groups. Herds of a dozen or so females are sometimes accompanied by an adult male. Although hierarchy exists in both male and female groups, ties are loose, and elands come and go. Nursery herds, often large groups, consist of females and calves of assorted ages.

Males tend to stay in one place. Sometimes as they grow older they become loners. Often they inhabit bush areas near water year-round. Being nonterritorial, bulls frequently meet. When they do, they rely on an order of rank, established by head-shoving and horn-wrestling contests when they were calves in a nursery herd. This dominance order precludes fighting, even over an estrous female.

A bull's status is enhanced by his massive neck and flapping dewlap and the conspicuous frontal brush of hair from forehead to nose. In displays of dominance the male sometimes rubs this brush in mud and urine and aggressively swings his horns through grass and brush.

The eland is oxlike, with its large body and relatively short lower limb segments. As it walks it makes a clicking sound, caused either

by tendons of its forelegs or by the splaying and coming together of its two-toed hoofs. Its trot is a seemingly tireless gait, at which it can travel long distances.

Less dependent on water than many hoofed mammals, elands can go for weeks at a time without drinking. They feed at night when browse as well as grass is dew laden. During the day they seek shade. Midday sweating, which normally keeps an eland's body temperature constant, ceases in drought conditions. Then panting dispels some body heat, while the rest of the several-degree rise in body temperature is stored until nighttime, when the air cools. Dry feces and highly concentrated urine indicate that moisture is being conserved.

Calves, concealed for the first two weeks after birth, depend on their mothers for only a short time. Soon they join nursery herds and form stronger bonds with other calves than with their mothers. This mutual attraction among calves causes the herds to number 30 or more youngsters, including yearlings. As the mother-calf bonds weaken, the cows leave the nursery group to associate with other females, but almost always there are a few adult females with the nursery herd to chase off hyenas, wild dogs, and even lions.

Aardvark

Aardvark is an Afrikaans word meaning "earth-pig." It is the name of an animal that has a long, narrow muzzle, piglike snout, donkeylike ears, humped back, and a thick tail that tapers to a point. Its powerful hind limbs and relatively short forelimbs have stout claws that are spadelike digging tools. There are no teeth in its muzzle, so the mobile snout is in fact a tube containing only thin bony plates. Stiff hairs surrounding the nostrils filter dust and even seal off nasal passages when the animal digs. Within the nose, fleshy tentacles heighten sensitivity to smell. Far back in the aardvark's skull and jaw are a variable number of small peg teeth. Unlike the teeth of other mammals, they are made of thin columns of dentine and have no enamel.

Termites and ants are the aardvark's food. Among these termites are the mound builders, whose termitaries are centers of aardvark activity. After a narrow hole is excavated in the mound's base, the digger thrusts its snout into the interior, flicking its sticky 40-centimeter- (16-inch-) long tongue into the nest galleries and ingesting its fill of swarming insects.

Well after dark the aardvark emerges from its hole to sniff its winding way over the savanna. Its fondness for termites means dependence on the grazing habits of hoofed mammals. Attracted to the grazers' dung piles, ground-living termites surface at night to feed on dry manure and trampled grass. The aardvark pauses, presses its nose to the ground, and then digs rapidly. A cache of dung balls containing larvae of scarab beetles is exhumed, and the larvae are consumed. Now and again the aardvark tests with its nose and swivels its ears for scent or sound of hyena, lion, or wild dog.

Alarmed by a predator at close range, an aardvark does a somersault and bellows. Usually its defense is to run for a hole and dig furiously, pelting dirt at its pursuer with each powerful hind-leg thrust.

By dawn the aardvark has returned to its hole or dug a new one. It seals up the entrance, leaving just a small opening, then curls, snout covered by tail and hind feet, to sleep. Within the almost-sealed burrow the animal's need for oxygen may be reduced by a slowing of its metabolism. Flies winging about the entrance hole indicate that the burrow is occupied.

Some aardvark burrows are veritable warrens, with eight or more entrances, various chambers, and interconnecting passageways that extend as deep as six meters (almost 20 feet) below ground.

Warthog

The expression "hightailing it" must come from the warthog's way of going. At a springy trot this long-legged pig carries its tail straight up, tuft waving over its taut, fat little rump. The faster the trot, the stiffer the tail. In tall grass its tail is a moving signpost, a small flag to be seen by other warthogs.

Three paired protuberances of dense skin, or "warts," protect the male's eyes and jaws in ritualized head duels, tusk-to-tusk and forehead-to-forehead shoving contests. Females have smaller knobs and their tusks (large, curved upper canine teeth and somewhat smaller lower canines) are not as flared as the male's.

There are also hardened pads, or callosities, on the warthog's forelegs. Even newborn piglets have these kneeling pads. On its knees—or, more correctly, on its carpal, or wrist, joints—a warthog moves along, grazing and scraping for roots and bulbs.

Savanna grasslands and open woodlands, usually where aardvarks live and dig their burrows, are habitats for these social, *diurnal* pigs. Groups (a sow with several young piglets, two to four yearlings) or a solitary boar often graze among zebras and topi and kongoni. The warthogs rely on alarm snorts of these taller sentinels, as well as on attendant oxpeckers, to warn them of danger.

Daytime is spent eating, with interruptions for wallowing and a few short rest periods. Warthogs are fond of rubbing on banks, termite mounds, or each other. When they go to drink they exhibit self-confidence. Unlike other prey animals that mill about before going to a river or water hole, warthogs trot purposefully to get their drinks.

By dark warthogs return to their holes, which are usually abandoned aardvark dens. The ground den is the focal point of a warthog's rather small home range. Not only is it a safe place for raising piglets, but, used as a bolt-hole, it deters pursuing predators. Piglets go to ground headfirst. To protect their vulnerable hind ends and because they are too large to turn about in the tunnel, adults back in. The entrance slopes down for about five feet, then branches into two or more spacious underground chambers, in which the warthogs huddle for warmth.

Nyala

Nyala are inhabitants of dense bush, riverine forest, and savanna grassland in southeastern Africa. The male is an especially handsome tragelaphine: dark, slaty brown, with orange-chestnut stockings and heavy fringes of black hairs on throat, undersides, and thighs, and a proud head carriage.

These antelopes have a ritualized courtship display. The male pursues the *estrous* female closely. With head close to her flank or shoulder, he shoves his chin over her back, his dewlap fringe brushing across her body in hairy domination. Then he halts. In this lateral display the long hairs of his spinal crest are elevated and his bushy tail is upturned to flag white.

Mountain Nyala

A small mountain-heather-covered region of southern Ethiopian hill country is home to the mountain nyala, an antelope unknown to science until the early 1900s.

Shaggy-coated and grayish chestnut in color, the mountain nyala is larger than its lowland relative. An old male usually leads a solitary existence. His heavy horns spread wide in two open spirals. A short, dark-brown mane continues along the back as a brown-and-white spinal crest.

83 Savannas

7 Predators and Scavengers

Forest, bush, savanna, and grassland *ecology* depends upon a balance of relationships. Sunlight supplies the basic energy that is stored in plants, consumed by *herbivores*—grazers and browsers—and passed on to predators (animals that kill) and *scavengers* (animals that feed on carcasses).

Herbivores (abundant in numbers and of many kinds) are held in check by carnivores (some half dozen kinds, their numbers relatively few), as well as by starvation, accidents, such as broken legs and drownings, diseases, and parasites.

Ecological separation is the rule among the carnivores, from the big cats (lion, leopard, and cheetah) and wild dogs and hyenas to smaller forms like bat-eared fox, genet, and mongoose. This separation is insured by differing habitat preferences, activity patterns, and in some instances by response to seasonal changes in food supply.

Hoofed mammals furnish nearly all food for the five large carnivores: lion, leopard, cheetah, hyena, and wild dog. Differences in how, when, and what they hunt make it possible for these predators to coexist. Their hunting strategies differ: the cheetah uses high-speed chase to capture small gazelles; the leopard relies on ambush; lions make powerful rushes and seize their prey. Hyenas and wild dogs, pack hunters that kill by harassment, hunt at different times. In addition to hunting for, attacking, and killing their own hoofed-animal *prey*, these predators locate and scavenge from animals that have died from malnutrition, disease, or accident. And most of them will rob another predator of its kill.

Prey animals respond appropriately to these different hunting strategies. A herd of zebras or wildebeests will allow lions to approach much closer than hyenas before they gallop off. They pay little attention to a single hyena or wild dog. Gazelles, sure of their own ability to run, allow hyenas to come relatively close before fleeing. A cheetah, even in the distance, is cause for wariness.

Hunting strategies depend upon social systems. Cheetahs and leopards are solitary cats, a fact that increases their success in stalk-and-rush hunting. Lions are social. Hyenas and wild dogs, the most social of all, depend upon pack formation for cooperative chasing and killing.

The jackal, the wild dog, and the bat-eared fox represent the dog family (the Canidae) in sub-Saharan Africa. Living in open areas, these long-legged carnivores rely on running to elude other predators. They are social, some more than others, and live as a family (or as a group of families) within a hunting range. Social interactions among canids are marked by expressive movements of mouth and ears, as well as by postural changes and tail wagging.

Jackal

Relying on its keen sense of smell, a jackal finds a flock of guinea-fowl. Their sleekly curved bodies of white-spangled blue-black feathers are glossy in the late-afternoon sunlight. Suddenly the jackal pounces and grabs a cackling bird.

Adaptable opportunists, jackals are omnivores. They make it their business to explore and exploit whatever food sources they come upon as they trot, singly or in pairs, through their home ranges. Frequent stops to sniff or to listen punctuate their travel. Insects are eaten, dung beetles and their larvae, locusts and crickets. Grass rats and other rodents and ground birds are also prey. Even plant food is consumed.

At a kill jackals are scavengers, but where small antelopes are numerous, they are highly efficient predators. They prey heavily on young gazelles. Hunting within their 1.6-square-kilometer (1-mile-square) territory, male and female collaborate. While one harasses the mother, the other runs down the fawn. If there are pups to feed, the parents return to the earth den, a series of interconnecting holes dug into a termitary or a renovated aardvark den, and regurgitate food.

Often there are year-old siblings to act as baby-sitters for the pups while the parents, mated for life, forage. By sharing food, grooming, and playing, jackal parents appear to encourage their offspring to stay at home until their second year. Patricia D. Moehlman, who has studied jackals in the Serengeti, finds that these stay-at-home juveniles, by protecting the litter from hyenas and raptors and helping to feed them, increase the pups' chances of survival. Even a hyena flees, tail between its legs, when a yapping jackal darts about, nipping at its hind end.

As scavengers, jackals are always alert to the spiraling of a vulture that signals a kill. Trotting over, they lurk, waiting for the chance to snatch morsels of meat. They also follow lions or leopards to pilfer meat after a kill is made, and they patrol wildebeest calving grounds in the Serengeti, feeding on afterbirths.

Wild Dog

Wild dogs are highly social, living in packs of ten or more. Nomads of the open plains and hilly wooded country, they stay in an area only while pups are less than three months old and too young to travel. Within the pack males outnumber females, but only the highest ranking male and female produce pups.

During the day the pack lies about in thickets or shaded grass. Most of the hunting is done at dusk and at dawn. A mark of wild dog sociality is the meet ceremony that precedes the hunt. The dogs approach one another in a slinking, menacing way that dissolves into a friendly encounter. They run together, twittering and begging, gestures of submission and appeasement. Excitement builds within the pack during this joining-up time.

Once prey is sighted, the pack approaches at a slow walk. Then, when the herd turns to flee, the dogs stream after it in flat-out pursuit, sounding their wailing hoot calls. Their marbled (black, tan, and white) bodies contrast boldly with the muted body colors of the herd animals. When a gazelle is singled out, team effort becomes important. Sharp cornering causes the lead dog to overshoot. A second dog cuts a corner to close in. Again the gazelle makes a sharp turn to elude its pursuer, only to run into a third dog. In seconds the three white-tipped tails attract the rest of the pack to the fallen gazelle.

Food is shared by the pack. As the dogs gather to eat there is whining, cringing, tail wagging, and submissive rolling over, all appeasement gestures. Sharp cutting teeth tear at the carcass. Meat is bolted with little or no chewing. Food, carried back in the adults' large stomachs, is regurgitated for the begging pups and the one or two adults that stayed behind to baby-sit while the pack hunted. Pups are fed by all the dogs in the kin group.

When hunting larger prey, like zebras, wild dogs hunt in the manner of hyenas. They test the herd, looking for a likely victim—any animal that stands out, listless or injured, and does not run with the others.

Bat-eared Fox

Enormous, black-tipped, batlike ears, a dark facial mask, a brushy tail, slim dark legs, and a sharp-pointed muzzle distinguish this diminutive fox. Hunting for insects that make up much of its diet, the bat-eared fox relies on acutely sensitive, reflector-equipped ears to detect faint underground scratching sounds of feeding dung-beetle larvae. Grasshoppers, crickets, lizards, snakes, eggs and nestling birds, and small rodents also are food for the fox.

Foraging, at dusk and dawn and during the night, is punctuated by bouts of rapid digging. Dirt flies as forelegs whirr. The fox pauses, ears forward and nose into hole, then digs again. A manure ball is exhumed and cracked open. The dung-beetle grub is eaten with a rapid chopping of the fox's high-cusped cheek teeth (four premolars and four molars on each side of upper and lower jaws).

Termites are another favorite food. Foxes leap and, with a snap of the jaw, seize their flying prey in midair or lick up wingless termites from the ground.

The little foxes dig shallow burrows or renovate springhare holes. A burrow has several entrances and is home to as many as ten foxes, two females and their litters and a male. They avoid midday heat in these cool shelters. Then, in the softer light of late afternoon, when shadows move, birds sound again, and rustling and scuttling is heard in thickets, foxes emerge from their dens to lie out in the cooling air.

The fox shows aggression with flattened ears, stiffly upheld tail, and snarling lips. Submissive gestures include rolling on the back with legs waving, tail wagging, and tongue licking. Play among young foxes involves much chasing and fleeing.

Alarm causes a bat-eared fox to crouch, head to ground, and flatten its huge ears laterally. Escape from a raptor overhead or a pursuing hyena depends on the fox's agility. It zigzags for cover, with large brush-tail flailing.

Viverrids

Resembling what is thought to have been the common ancestral carnivore, the *viverrids* (civet, genet, and mongoose) are all relatively small. Their *dentition* is relatively unspecialized. Cheek teeth are not reduced in numbers nor are they realigned to suit any particular eating habits.

In Africa this group fills carnivore niches that on other continents are occupied by carnivores from other families. The mongoose is a long-bodied, short-legged weasel-like hunter. The genet is a catlike stalker. The civet in many ways parallels the raccoon.

Civet

Scent is important to civets. Following well-marked trails through thick cover, these high-rumped carnivores forage at night. A black facial mask and black marbling of the tawny gray coat make for eye-catching visibility in low light. Except at mating time, civets avoid one another. When confrontations occur, each animal increases its apparent body size by erecting the long hairs on its back and tail, a process accompanied by explosive coughs and growling.

Civets are adaptable. They eat both animal and plant foods and they live in various habitats: forests, reed beds, tall-grass savannas, and dense scrub. Their feeding habits are raccoonlike. Virtually anything is food. Around villages they are scavengers and raid gardens and chicken coops. And like the raccoon, they do some of their feeding in marshes and along streams.

A den in a termitary, tree hollow, rock crevice, or beneath tree roots is used by the female with cubs. Otherwise a civet sleeps wherever daybreak finds it, rotating resting sites within its home range. Males define their territories, which presumably overlap those of several females, by conspicuous fecal deposits and by scent smears. Large under-the-tail glands secrete a pungent musk that has been used by the perfume industry for centuries.

Genet

In wooded habitats from deep forest to forest-savanna margins to woodland and savanna and in drier thicket tangles of thornbush lives the small, lithe, long-bodied genet. It has a dark-spotted coat of soft, yellowish fur, a dark spinal stripe of erectile hairs, distinct facial markings, a long, ringed tail, and catlike retractile claws. Not only does the genet's climbing ability facilitate its escape into trees, but it also makes possible the exploiting of food sources and shelters that are above the reach of strictly ground-living mammals.

The darker forest genets, smooth-coated and small-spotted, patrol tree-canopy limbs at night in search of roosting birds, eggs, and nestlings. Daytime finds them sleeping in hollow trees. Blotched genets, larger-spotted and shorter-legged, live in forest and woodland habitats. They race with abandon along thin branches and den for the day in termitaries as well as in tree trunks. The common genet inhabits dry bush and woodland areas, spending much of its time on the ground. At night it is a stealthy hunter, prowling in thickets for small mammals. For all its grace in motion, the genet is an awkward killer, often falling on its side, clawing and kicking as it chews on its victim's head and neck.

Genets are solitary. Their social life, such as it is, depends upon scent-gland-conveyed information. Females appear to have territories, which they mark by scratching and by a pungent anal-gland secretion. Males are thought to wander more widely. But these are conjectures about the genet's social system, based on capture and release of poultry-stealing animals.

Mongoose

Agile animals with slender, grizzled-gray bodies, short legs, and long-haired tails, mongooses explore their usually dense habitat in pairs or alone. Some of them are skillful climbers, but for the most part mongooses are terrestrial. Their walking is interrupted by probing in crevices and holes and overturning rocks. When a mouse is happened upon, it is killed with a lightning-fast neck bite. Reptiles and ground-nesting birds and their eggs are also eaten. Eggs are grasped in the mongoose's five-fingered, curved-clawed forepaws and hurled backwards between its hind legs to crack open against tree trunk or rock. Dung piles attract mongooses. They consume the beetles and dig for larvae.

Mongooses are tail followers. This habit starts when young follow their mother, her scent-gland secretion being an adhesive enabling the cubs to maintain contact along narrow tunnels in deep grass. As adults, foraging in pairs or groups, one mongoose follows just behind the other, sounding little contact calls.

Pairs are playful. Tail switching invites pursuit as one mongoose zigzags in front of the other, flicking its fluffed tail from side to side.

Depending upon the species, mongooses are either diurnal or nocturnal. They den in ground holes, termitaries, rock crevices, and hollow logs, sleeping with head tucked under the belly.

Spotted Hyena

A large head, powerful forequarters, sloping back, dark-spotted yellowish-gray coat, a mood-expressing tail, and an awkward loping gallop identify the hyena. By day it is a scavenger, often foraging alone and watching for the descent of vultures to locate a carcass. Its scavenging reputation comes from association with vultures on kills, for this is the way hyenas are most often seen.

Neck muscles, as well as chewing muscles, are well developed. A leg or even a whole carcass may be carried off or cached in a nearby water hole. Scrambling at the carcass, each hyena swallows large quantities of food. Hyenas are rapid eaters. Incisor and canine teeth are used to pull off chunks of meat. A shearing mechanism, formed by an upper premolar and a lower molar at the back of the jaws, severs tough skin and tendons. Bones are splintered and chewed by blunt, crushing premolars, three on each side of upper and lower jaw.

Soon all that remains is the skull and that, too, is chewed. The hyena's digestive physiology, like its dentition, is specialized. Bone is completely digested in the stomach so that hyena feces consist of fine white powder.

Wildebeests, zebras, and gazelles are hyena prey, and each species is hunted differently. Gazelle hunting, often done in daylight, is usually a one-hyena pursuit. There is a chase and some sharp cornering; then the hyena grabs and disembowels its victim. Hans Kruuk, an ethologist who has lived among hyenas, estimates that a hyena has a one-in-three chance of running down a gazelle.

By night, when their melancholy *whoo-oop* calls sound, hyenas are pack hunters. Wildebeest-hunting involves careful selection of prey. One hyena approaches the herd, then runs into it, scattering the animals. The hyena halts and looks over the running wildebeests. Suddenly it gives chase, and other hyenas join in pursuit. When the exhausted wildebeest stops to confront the pack, it is grabbed, pulled down, and devoured.

Pack cooperation is also necessary when zebras are hunted. A family group (a stallion with his mares and their foals) is found. As the hyenas approach, mares and foals bunch together and walk away. The stallion rushes at the pack, chasing one and then another with teeth and striking forefeet. Confusion results. A mare barks and the family gallops off, hyenas in pursuit. After a short chase one of the zebras is grabbed, brought to a halt, and surrounded by the pack.

Social organization is a fact of hyena life. Groups called clans consist of hyenas that know each other. Clan members have solitary pursuits but come together to hunt as a pack or to defend their territory. When a clan regroups all members take part in the ritualized meeting ceremony.

Each clan (of 30 to 80 hyenas) occupies a large, well-defined territory. Neighboring clans also have their territories.

Patrolling clan members maintain boundaries by pasting analgland secretion on grass clumps, rocks, or logs, and by defecating and scratching. Clashes sometimes occur when a kill is made on the boundary. As hyenas contest the carcass there is turmoil, accompanied by weird giggles, yells, and wails.

The den, usually a system of underground tunnels enlarged by the hyenas from another animal's burrow and having several entrance holes, is the center of clan activity. It is here that the dominance of the females, conspicuously larger and more powerful than the males, is apparent. Males are kept from the den area. Cubs, black when very young, then spotted like the adults, run and chase, playful like all young carnivores.

Aardwolf

A shy inhabitant of dry, open plains and thorn scrub, the aardwolf has specialized eating habits. It feeds mostly on termites and insect larvae. Its jaws are weak and its cheek teeth are much reduced and widely spaced. Long-legged and striped (dark brown on yellowish buff), this *hyaenid* has a bushy black-tipped tail, a head-to-tail mane that, when erected, makes it look twice its normal size, leathery muzzle and lips, large eyes, and huge ears. The aardwolf forages singly or sometimes in pairs.

Usually it is after dark when harvester termites, plentiful where there has been heavy grazing, surface from their underground nests. The aardwolf locates prey primarily by hearing and then scenting. Once found, termites are lapped up. The tongue, coated with sticky saliva to which the termites adhere, moves out and in over spadelike lower incisor teeth. In hyena fashion, an aardwolf drops to its knees (actually its wrist joints) to gorge. Only soldier termites, whose pointed heads secrete a distasteful chemical, are left behind. After feasting an aardwolf may stay denned for two days, sleeping off a meal that is rich in protein and fat.

Aardwolves make use of natural holes, dig their own dens, or more often take over abandoned aardvark burrows. Both sexes paste mark, or identify by smears of anal-gland secretion, prominent landmarks within their home ranges. Middens (patches of bare ground used for defecating) also are paste-marked. Smaller smears are laid on grass stems to mark areas previously foraged during the night.

The Smaller Cats: Caracal and Serval

Agility and lightning-fast reflexes make the slender, sandy-colored caracal an efficient hunter. Stalking a flock of guinea-fowl or sandgrouse, a caracal can bat down several birds in a single pounce. Usually it hunts in late afternoon or at night. It relies on surprise and instant attack. Along streams and in fringe areas between woodland and open plains it finds rodents and other small prey.

All *felids* (members of the cat family) use ears for expression. When they meet they usually sit and look at each other, turning away often and flicking their ears. The caracal's long, tuft-tipped ears emphasize its moods. Alertness and confidence are signaled by erect ears. Tension or defensiveness are indicated by ears drawn back.

Where longer rainy seasons produce taller grass cover, the caracal is replaced by the serval, a long-necked and long-legged spotted cat that sometimes leaps above the grass tops in order to see better. As it pushes through cover, listening for prey, its large ears are rotated independently. The rustling activity of rodents elicits a rush from the crouched cat. The victim is seized with the claws and killed with a neck bite. When a bird is found, the serval pounces, leaping vertically and striking with its forepaws.

Cats are the most effective killers of all the carnivores. They hunt mostly by sight. Clawing into their prey, they bite with accuracy and usually bring about a quick death. Although their killing techniques

vary, all of them have a steeply sloped face and short muzzle, canine teeth that are long, sharp, and recurved for seizing prey, and narrow, sharp-bladed cheek teeth for shearing and cutting flesh. For some of these lithe-bodied, well-muscled carnivores claws are climbing tools as well as meat hooks.

Visual and olfactory and sometimes vocal signals are important in feline communication. The three big cats—lion, leopard, and cheetah—are intolerant of one another. Except for the lion, the cats are solitary, each with a hunting range that overlaps those of its neighbors.

Lion

Lions are social. Most of them live in *prides,* groups of about 15 that have their own exclusive home ranges or pride areas. The females in a pride are all related. Males, nomads for a time after they leave the security of their mothers' prides, later join other prides as adults. Nomads associate in groups of two to four. Their home ranges overlap and they move amicably from one partner or group to another.

Pride members do not always stay together. Where prey is mainly gazelles, the brownish-yellow females frequently go off in twos and threes. Larger groups form where wildebeests and zebras are numerous.

The pride's integrity is maintained by the females' hostility toward other females. The males—larger, darker, heavier-bodied, and handsomely maned—drive off male interlopers. Usually two to four in a

pride, the males patrol and mark the pride area by urine spraying, rubbing heads in bushes, and defecating, and proclaim their territory by roaring—eight or nine roars that echo and throb, followed by grunts. Grunting also serves to maintain contact as the pride moves from place to place. The male's mane, so conspicuous in outline, probably serves for recognition and avoidance of male encounters. The mane also is protection from teeth and claws when fights occur.

Lions hunt by sight and sound, usually during the night or at dusk or dawn. Sometimes they hunt along river courses in daytime or lie in wait to ambush hoofed animals that come to drink.

Mostly lions hunt by stalking—creeping forward and freezing, making use of any available cover. Then they rely on surprise, a burst of speed, and their own strength. A single paw smash kills smaller prey. Hunting in a pride, or communal hunting, increases the rate of success in killing larger animals, but many hunts end in failure. Females do most of the hunting. They fan out, then crouch, bellies to the ground. Tall grass, a termitary, or a rock are used to conceal their stalk. Then comes the rush. In bounds of 10 to 12 feet a female overtakes the wildebeest, hooks its rump with a grappling forepaw-hook, and brings it down. Another grabs the neck to strangle the antelope, or seizes its nose in her mouth to make the kill by suffocation.

The males then appear, drive off the females, and feed. Cubs come to feed with them, and the females return. There is much quarreling and snarling among the feeding lions, and little tolerance is shown the cubs.

Lions in Ngorongoro Crater have adopted a strategy of easy hunting. They rely on one of the resident hyena packs to make its kill. Then, attracted by the cacophony, they rush in, bowl over the hyenas, and claim their kill.

99

Occasionally a male lion makes a kill. An eland is consumed by the pride in a few hours. Then the pride lolls about in the shade of a thicket to sleep off a feast that satisfies them for several days. While the big lions doze, small cubs chase and stalk, pounce and wrestle, ambush and chew on the tips of flicking tails. Play perfects their skills for hunting. Cubs trail their mother at three months but do not participate in hunts until they are almost a year old.

Leopard

A solitary inhabitant of riverine forests, dense brush around water holes, thickets, and rock-strewn ravines, the leopard spends its day in a tree, draped along a horizontal limb, dozing. Dark spots arranged in rosettes on its tawny coat merge with the pattern of sunlight filtering through leaves. The leopard is an agile climber. It can leap three meters (almost ten feet) up into a tree and descend head first. It is also capable of horizontal leaps that span up to six meters (nearly twenty feet). Kopjes are also used for daytime resting and watching. As ethologist George B. Schaller has noted, the leopard leads "a remarkably self-contained existence."

Usually it is dusk when the leopard stirs. Mostly a nighttime hunter, it still relies on cover and stealthy stalking to get within close striking distance of its prey. Eyes fixed on a tail-flicking gazelle and body lowered almost to the ground, it stalks with a snakelike motion. A quick rush and a claws-extended strike flip the gazelle. Grasping with its claws, the leopard makes a fatal, spine-dislocating bite at neck or base of skull. Power rather than speed and stamina is the leopard's hunting asset.

To protect its kill from marauding hyenas, wild dogs, or lions, the leopard grasps the carcass by the neck, its forelegs straddling the body, drags it to a tree, scrambles it up, and with some struggle, drapes it over a limb or wedges it in a fork. This way a Thomson's gazelle lasts for two or three nights. The leopard is an economical predator, killing about half as many prey animals as a cheetah. Even when driven from its kill by hyenas or wild dogs, a leopard may charge back, seize the carcass, and haul it up a tree trunk for safekeeping.

Leopards are adaptable, a fact of life that bodes well for their future. Their food varies according to what is available in their range. Warthogs, hyraxes, dik-diks, hares, rodents, ground birds, baboons, and even insects are eaten. Richard Estes shared the use of a tree platform he built for observing wildebeests in Ngorongoro Crater with a female leopard whose favorite prey was jackals. Often she carried her victim up onto the platform to bat about in cat-and-mouse fashion before making a killing bite.

Male leopards are territorial. Their five- to twenty-square-mile ranges are spaced to overlap the ranges of several females. Except at mating time or when cubs accompany their mother, mutual avoidance is the rule. Tree-scratching, ground-scraping, and urine-spraying are used for communication, as is the rasping coughlike call.

Cheetah

Long-limbed and slender-bodied, the cheetah is made for speed. Its small, rounded head has a black tear-stripe that runs from the inner corner of each eye to the angle of the mouth. Predator ecologists George and Lory Frame learned to recognize individuals by photographing facial spot patterns. Then, in their words, they "watched and waited while the ripples spread in the rings of a cheetah's existence—the sleeping, walking, hunting, and eating that makes up its life."*

Early morning and late afternoon are times for hunting small antelopes, hares, and ground birds. Like the leopard, the cheetah preys heavily on Thomson's gazelles. Here again ecological separation is apparent. Cheetahs hunt in open plains, while leopards require thick cover and do most of their hunting at night.

The hunting cheetah walks along, stopping now and again to look about. When a herd of gazelles is sighted the cheetah stops, tenses,

---

*George and Lory Frame, *Swift and Enduring: Cheetahs and Wild Dogs in the Serengeti* (New York, Dutton, 1981), p. 7.

lowers its head. If the gazelles are unaware of its approach, the cheetah makes short stealthy runs, interrupted by motionless pauses, until it is within chasing range. If the gazelles detect its presence, the cheetah walks openly in their direction. A third approach technique, used in tall grass or scattered bush, is stalking. Then the cheetah inches forward, its belly almost on the ground.

When it is 50 to 60 yards from the gazelles, the cheetah rushes. All at once gazelles are everywhere. As the herd flees, a gazelle is singled out. The spotted cat is a blur of motion. Its long, thick-furred, ringed, white-tipped tail is a rudderlike counterbalance as the cheetah keeps pace with the gazelle's swerves and double-backs. In a short, 70-miles-per-hour sprint the cat overtakes the gazelle and uses a forepaw to hook a leg, or with a sharp dewclaw snags the hindquarters. Once toppled, the gazelle is pinned down, seized by the throat, and strangled.

For all its dazzling sprinting speed, the cheetah does not always kill. As Jonathan Kingdon watched, a fleeing impala executed a sideways leap to avoid colliding with his motionless vehicle. Lacking the antelope's agility, the chasing cheetah slipped up behind and skidded on its side and nearly collided with the car.

In addition to gazelles and impalas, other small and medium-sized ungulates as well as calves and foals of larger hoofed animals are prey. Standing and panting over a young zebra just killed is a king cheetah, a mutant form with longer, softer hair and large marbled spots. Its feeding companion's shorter coat is marked by the normal round black spots.

Once a kill is made the cheetah must feed quickly, before vultures attract lions, hyenas, or jackals. The cheetah has blunt, doglike claws so it cannot haul its prey up into a tree. Nor with its relatively weak jaws and teeth is it able to defend a kill from marauders. Because it is often robbed of its kills, the cheetah must hunt and kill frequently.

Cheetahs are often seen alone, hunting or stretched out in a thicket or in the grass. Lying on its narrow-bodied side, with head raised, ears lowered, high-set eyes peering intently through the grass, a cheetah is almost invisible. By hiding, this fleet runner avoids confrontations with other predators.

Cheetahs are aloof. Their greetings consist of sniffing or a brief cheek rub. Even their grooming is purposeful, done when faces are bloodstained from feeding or coats are rain soaked. Spray-marking, though it does not appear to define individual home ranges, is a cheetah's means of communication. In some areas cheetahs have discernable, overlapping home ranges. In the Serengeti they follow the ungulate migration, moving with their favorite prey, the Thomson's gazelles.

Three or four cubs are born, usually in a dense thicket. Eyes are sealed and the tiny, dark bodies are covered by a mantle of long, bluish-white hair. For the first months of life this mantle may protect the cub, because it resembles the broad, silvery back of the ratel, or honey badger, an aggressive little carnivore that predators avoid because of its musky odor. The mother moves her cubs frequently. Whickering calls greet her return from hunting. At night she suckles and grooms her cubs.

At two months of age, cubs move with their mother, sharing her kills and bedding at night where they happen to be. This is a time of danger, when cub mortality is high. It is also a time for learning. Sometimes inept cubs spoil their mother's hunting success. When prey is captured the female often leaves her victim barely alive so that cubs learn to kill. There is also time for play—games of stalk, pounce, and "king of the termite mound."

Cubs have a long period of dependence, staying with their mother until they are 17 months old. After leaving their mother, young cheetahs often stay together in sibling groups.

Loss of habitat, changing conditions, intolerance to humans and their grazing herds threaten the cheetah, whose numbers are dwindling. Even tourism is a factor. The Frames found cheetahs killing at midday because their morning hunts were too frequently disrupted by game viewers.

Vulture

Scavenging, the task of cleaning up at a death site, is the role of many animals. Vultures are daytime scavengers, replaced at night by jackals, hyenas, and sometimes lions.

Flying distances of up to 700 kilometers (nearly 100 miles) in a day to locate their widely scattered food sources, vultures take advantage of air movements to keep themselves aloft. They use thermal updrafts

to gain altitude. Then, wings open, they glide, gradually losing altitude until they reach another upcurrent. Soaring expends relatively little energy, so these scavengers can follow the migratory ungulate herds throughout the year. Their food supply is constant except during the rainy season, when there are no thermal updrafts. Then vultures go for days without feeding.

Often vultures are first in line where an animal has succumbed from disease or injury. They plummet down where a cheetah, or hyenas, or lions have made a kill. The descent of one vulture is a signal to all other vultures in sight. Even those soaring farther away from the food source notice the change in flight behavior and converge on the site. Within an hour there may be a hundred or more birds congregated on the carcass.

While larger species like Ruppell's griffon vulture and the white-backed vulture wait for midmorning updrafts to fly, the smaller hooded vulture arrives early, often early enough to harass a still-feeding hyena or lion.

Scaly feet down, a vulture brakes with wings and tail and bounces onto the grass where other vultures are feeding. Neck arched and wings outspread, the newcomer leaps into the air and moves in to feed. Flapping, gabbling, and hissing ensues. Soon the carcass is the center of a crowd of twenty vultures. On the carcass are the dominant birds. Surrounding them are subdominant vultures, hungry but wait-

ing their turn. Outside this circle are clusters of vultures that have already fed, less aggressive than the famished newcomers.

Some vultures, like the lappet-faced, have a powerful hooked beak and a rachetlike tongue for ripping open a carcass and tearing off pieces of skin and sinew. Others feed on softer flesh and intestines, while those with long, snakelike heads and necks reach deep inside the body cavity. A large crop enables the birds to gorge and then fly off to cliffside nests or treetop roosts. Whatever their specialty, vultures are rapid and efficient consumers of carrion that otherwise would litter the plains.

Birds and mammals are not the only scavengers. As soon as a carcass is torn open, dung beetles fly in to land. They gather up and roll balls of half-digested grass from the dead animal's stomach, in which they lay their eggs. Fly-maggots and bacteria soon are at work on tough skin and tendons. Hornworm moths lay their eggs on the horns. When the caterpillars hatch out, they devour the hairlike substance of the horn sheaths. These small sanitary engineers work so diligently that in a matter of days all that is left of a hoofed-animal kill is the bleached skull with bare horn cores.

8 The Grasslands

Africa is a land of sky. Cumulus clouds, billowing, weightless, and ever-changing, tower up in the afternoon sky and travel with the southeast wind. Sometimes they catch on hills and hang around them, or snag on a high peak and break into a rain shower. More often they sail high on a westward course. Where bush and savanna give way to rolling grassland, clouds cast shadows over a sea of grasses, turned from green to the tawny hue of a lion's haunch. During the dry season mirages form. At water's edge these shining lakes disappear, leaving white clay soil and a distant shimmering illusion.

As the sun crosses the equator on its spring passage to the Northern Hemisphere, it pulls damp air inland from the Indian Ocean. Clouds become lower and thicker. Thunder sounds. Rain comes and with it the smell of settling dust, washed trees, and newly wet grass. Late in the afternoons, for six to eight weeks, it rains. Clear water runs in gullies, trees sprout new leaves and silvery thorns, and grass becomes green.

Lush grass growth marks ancient swamps and lakes that once covered the floor of the Great Rift Valley and dotted the Serengeti Plains. The grasses are of many kinds, the dominant ones determined by soil type. Heads of red oat grass give a russet-gold color to some sweeps of grassland. Star grasses flourish on the fertile, well-drained soil of old termite mounds and abandoned *manyatta* sites where herdspeople lived in mud-plastered huts, their livestock protected at night by a circle of thorny branches. Guinea grasses grow tall in moist areas. Bristle grasses cover valley floors.

Grasses survive the withering effects of the dry season either by having fleshy roots or by holding over in seeds. When the rains come, the grasses respond. In a competition to cover the ground, some grow tall. Others spread by rhizomes, underground runners that produce shoots. Still others spring up from seeds on bare patches. The mat-forming grasses depend on being grazed. Clipped short by the muzzles of hoofed mammals, they spread out and grow quickly. If grazers do not come, these grasses are choked out by taller competitors.

Abundance of grass supports incredible numbers of ungulate grazers, each species ecologically separated from the others. A classic example of this separation is the zebra/topi and wildebeest/Thomson's gazelle grazing succession. Zebras, with upper as well as lower incisor teeth, can crop tough grass stems. In fact they prefer this roughage. While blunt-muzzled wildebeests graze on horizontal leaves, the slender-nosed topi reach for leftover lower stems. Following this mowing, tiny-muzzled Tommies nibble new grass that sprouts from clipped bases of the stems.

Kob

A handsome, reddish-colored, medium-sized antelope, the male kob has a muscular neck and thick, lyre-shaped horns that bend back in a double curve. He has a white throat chevron, white eye rings that give him a gentle expression, and a white belly. The fronts of his legs are marked with black.

Like other grazers, kobs often are attracted to the sweet-tasting grasses that grow on the fertile, well-drained termite mounds. Termitaries are also lookout posts. Their air-shaft chimneys are used for rubbing by many of the plains animals, until gradually they are worn down and the rich packed mortar returns to the soil.

Herds of 20 to 40 kobs share their short-grass pastures with buffalo, hippo, hartebeest, topi, and warthog. Most of their range is in Uganda, where local populations are often dense. Unlike their reedbuck relatives, which are attached to certain places, kobs often gather

and move considerable distances from one grazing ground to another. Water is always nearby.

In grassland areas where kob numbers are high, males maintain year-round breeding territories, or *leks*. Year after year they trample circular areas, each 30 to 50 meters (98 to 164 feet) in diameter and bare at the center. A lek contains 30 to 40 of these circular land holdings. In this cluster of defended territories the males are preoccupied with fighting, chasing, and displaying. Head and neck high, they prance on stiff legs, flashing their black foreleg markings.

Females wander in herds around the lek. When an estrous female is attracted by the display antics of the males, she moves purposefully toward the center of the lek, ignoring the attentions of peripheral males. She mates with one of three or four males that occupy the most hotly contested central territories. Then, as she makes her way back to the female herd, she may also mate with other males in the lek.

Where kob herds are more mobile, the males establish their territories at a checkpoint on a ridge, near a termitary, or on an open area of good grazing, anywhere the herd's movement is slowed.

So strenuous is all this activity in the lek that a replacement system is apparent. As the central males become exhausted, peripheral males take over their holdings. Sooner or later even the young males loitering in bachelor groups gain entry on the edges of the lek.

White Rhinoceros

Long, narrow head, broad muzzle, tapering nasal horn with massive squarish base, close-set, hair-tipped, tubular ears, nuchal (neck) hump, and straight topline interrupted by a presacral as well as a sacral (pelvic) hump distinguish the white rhino. A placid beast, it is usually easy to approach, and it is much larger than its black-rhino relative. Actually its color is only slightly lighter than the black rhino's. *White* is thought to have come from the Boer *weit,* referring to the wide upper lip.

White rhinos are found in two widely separated areas. In southern Africa, where they were once numerous throughout the bushveld (wooded grassland), some 3,000 are now restricted to reserves and national parks. Their northern range includes tree-savanna habitat in the Sudan, west of the Nile, where their numbers have plummeted from 800 in 1979 to 400 in 1980 to 12 in 1982. They also are found in parts of Zaire, Chad, and the Central African Republic. In the 1960s a small number of white rhinos were reintroduced in northwestern Uganda. Most, if not all of them, were slaughtered during conflict between Tanzanian and Ugandan troops in the late 1970s. In Kenya's Meru National Park, white rhinos translocated from South Africa are protected from poachers by armed guards.

The white rhino is a grazer. With no functional incisor teeth, it uses the hardened pad of lower lip against squared upper lip to crop grass. Compared to the black rhino it has high-crowned cheek teeth. White rhinos tend to be fat, which may be why their skin folds are less conspicuous than those of a black rhino.

When grazing, the head hangs almost vertically. Raising the heavy head, something a white rhino always appears reluctant to do, causes constriction of neck muscles and ligament and makes the fat-padded nuchal hump even more prominent. The rhino moves with head carried low, trotting briskly at speeds up to 24 kilometers (15 miles) per hour. Impelled by hind feet rapidly striking the ground, it gallops head down for short sprints at 40 kilometers (25 miles) per hour.

White rhinos associate in groups of two and three, sometimes in groups of ten to fourteen. Good grazing brings together still larger numbers. They tend to be sedentary. Eight to 12 hectares (20 to 30 acres) is wet-season home range size. Dry-season conditions cause rhinos to wander more widely. Males occupy territories defined by urine spraying on tall grass tufts and dung scattering and defended in ritualized boundary confrontations with other bulls. Cows have over-lapping ranges and move freely through the territories of six or more bulls. Often a fight over an estrous female results in bloodshed.

Rhinos graze heavily in the early morning. Midday is rest time, when shade of a tree or termite mound is sought. There they stand for a time, then lie down, feet folded beneath them. Sometimes they stand on a ridge where breezes ward off biting flies. In the afternoon they move off to drink and then wallow in mud. By late afternoon it is time to graze again.

A rhino calf is born after 17 months' gestation. Its tiny horn nub-bins are covered by dark membranes and it has sparse black body hairs. Unlike a black-rhino calf, which follows close on its mother's heels, the white-rhino calf usually takes the lead, sometimes guided by nudges and prods of its mother's long nasal horn. When separated from its mother, a rhino calf squeals. It will suckle for more than a year. The cow-calf bond, a protective mechanism that prevents the calf from straying and perhaps being killed by hyenas, lions, or wild dogs, is so strong that calves have been known to stand by their dead mothers for as long as a week, chasing off vultures.

Ground Hornbill

A male ground hornbill snaps up a lizard, drops it, then snatches it up again before swallowing it head first. These turkey-sized black birds strut over grassland and savanna in pairs or family groups, scanning the ground for mice, nestling birds, reptiles, insects, and even fruit. Males have red skin on face and throat; females have red or blue throat skin. Their large bills are actually bony networks filled with air spaces.

Ground hornbills often feed on insects stirred up by grazing animals. Taking advantage of this trusting association between hoofed animals and hornbills, native hunters once draped skins of the dead birds, head and neck intact, over their own heads. Then, imitating the bird's foraging movements, they would crawl in disguise to within spearing distance of their antelope quarry.

Springhare

The springhare, a rabbit-sized rodent that lives in flat, short-grass habitats, has short forelimbs, long powerful hindlimbs, and a long, black, brush-tufted tail. It is a *bipedal* animal that uses its hind feet for hopping and seldom touches its forefeet to the ground. When frightened, the springhare changes from kangaroolike hops to explosive, zigzagging leaps up to three meters (not quite ten feet) in length.

Hopping habits are reflected in the springhare's anatomy. Femur and tibia (long bones of the hind limb) are stout levers served by large muscles. The spines of its sacral vertebrae are peculiarly shaped to provide increased muscle-attachment area. In midleap a springhare's body is cantilevered between its hip joints, the anterior part counterbalanced by muscles and the heavy brush of the tail. Propulsion comes from the stout, strong-nailed third toe, flanked by second and fourth toes, of the hind feet.

Like other *saltatorial* (hopping) rodents, the springhare has enlarged *auditory bullae* (bony chambers of the inner ear). Their inflation, which displaces all the bones at the back of the skull, probably functions for balance as well as for amplification of ground vibrations that reveal a predator's approach. When the springhare rests in its usual rolled position, the flat top of its head, pushed between its big hind feet, lies directly on the ground.

Springhare burrows, their openings often sealed by daytime occupants, dot the dry, sandy soil of Crescent Island in Kenya's Lake Naivasha. Deep inside the burrows, protected from sun and safe from predators, the springhares sleep, singly or sometimes in pairs, each with one offspring. Well after dark they emerge to feed on stems and sprouts of grasses, dig up grass roots, and eat a few insects. Then their eyes reflect bright red in the beam of a flashlight.

Thomson's Gazelle

Herds of small, yellow-brown Thomson's gazelles with bold, black flank stripes, white bellies, and ever-whisking tails amble and graze here and there on the short-grass plains. Those in the distance are visible only when they turn their white rumps. Now and then a gazelle nods its head on one side, daintily anointing the tip of a grass stem with the sticky secretion from his facial gland; such territorial marking occupies much of a male gazelle's time. Tommies or, more correctly, Thomson's gazelles are named in honor of Scottish geologist

Joseph Thomson, leader of an 1883 expedition to Kenya.

Being small (about two feet at the shoulder) and filling the plain as they often do, Tommies rely on open habitat for safety. Even their incessant tail wagging is a habit that pertains to their well-being. "When one gazelle does not see any more tails flicking out of the corner of its eye, it is time to be elsewhere."*

Wildebeests, plains zebras, and elands are frequently the Tommies' grazing companions. In fact the gazelles rely on these larger ungulates to graze and trample the taller grasses, making more accessible the tiny shoots they prefer. Grass fires, which occur as the plains are drying out, result in fresh green growth. But as the dry season progresses, larger hoofed animals—wildebeests, zebras, and elands—move to woodland areas to share a year-round water supply and better grazing conditions with buffaloes and impalas. Tommies, reluctant to move from the vast short-grass plains, are last to leave.

---

*Norman Myers, *The Long African Day,* p. 33.

Grant's Gazelle

A tawny gazelle, larger than the Tommie, with long horns and a conspicuous rectangular white rump patch bordered by a vertical black thigh stripe is named for James Augustus Grant, who accompanied John Hanning Speke on his search for the sources of the Nile.

Grant's gazelles live in scrubby semidesert areas, as well as in open savannas and grasslands. They are migrants where food supply changes with seasons, residents where it is adequate throughout the year. Except during early wet season, when there is fresh green grass, these gazelles are browsers on shrubs and herbs. As they feed, side-to-side tail switching maintains herd contact.

There are female—or nursery—herds, bachelor groups, and often mixed herds. Dominant males have territories. Their encounters are ritualized. Head-tilting is followed by face-to-face confrontation, heads back and necks bulging, or two males may pretend to graze and then paw or thrash their horns in the grass. Sometimes horns are clashed.

A female, her fawn hidden in tall grass, grazes some distance away but is watchful for cheetahs and wild dogs. If a baboon or other small predator happens on her fawn, she will rush to its defense. She will continue to harass the predator if the fawn is killed.

Ostrich

Largest of living birds, the ostrich is a *cursorial* omnivore. It wanders over the grassland and through the thornbush on long, powerful, featherless legs. Each foot has one large toe and an outer small toe, a condition that suggests the ostrich is in the evolutionary process of becoming a single-toed runner. Usually ostriches travel in bands of 10 to 50. As they run, the surging movement of many legs is blurred. Top speed is about 48 kilometers (30 miles) per hour. An ostrich can outrun a lion's rush. Fleeter predators are wary of the bird's ripping strikes and fierce pecks.

Ostriches often consort with zebras and other hoofed animals, an association that works to mutual advantage. The ostriches, being so tall, are lookout sentinels. The grazers stir up insects and send lizards scuttling and snakes slithering for the birds. Like many plains and bush animals, ostriches bathe in dust, then fluff and preen their feathers.

Ostrich eggs, ten or more, are laid in a shallow, scraped nest. Both male and female share in the incubating process. If the nest is a communal one, there are two or three females to take turns. Their

less conspicuous dull gray plumage is adapted for daytime sitting. The male, with black body, white wing feathers, and pink legs, takes the night shift.

Hyenas, and sometimes baboons, pilfer ostrich eggs. The Egyptian vulture uses a stone-casting technique to break the hard, shiny, pitted shell so it can guzzle the contents. If a jackal or a mongoose comes along, the ostrich leaves the nest area and distracts the predator with a broken-wing display, fluttering the huge flight feathers of one wing, faltering and staggering.

Hatching occurs over several days, but it is not long before all the gray, down-covered chicks are strutting awkwardly about the nest area. Soon mottled plumage replaces their down and the chicks accompany their tall parents, heads up and legs twinkling, in compact formation.

African Buffalo

Black silhouettes of massive ironlike animals form clumps along the lakeshore. A bull raises his head with a snort and turns to stare with lashed eyes and sniff with leathery nose. The other buffaloes, grazing in the marsh, suddenly explode and thunder off, a mass of running and bucking forms.

Once they are out on open grassland the herd bunches and wheels about. Heads high, the buffaloes watch and test the wind for scent of the predators that caused alarm. Because of their bulk, older bulls are always at the rear of a stampeding herd. Several of them leave the group and move back toward the marsh, flushing several lions that had been crouching in the tall grass.

When lions prey on buffaloes it is usually an old bull that is killed. Bellowing, jumping, and twisting as claws rake his tough hide, an ambushed buffalo often escapes serious injury by lions. As one lion falls to the ground, winded, the other is tossed high by the massive horns.

Horns are used in social interaction as well as for defense. There is daily jabbing, hooking, and jostling for grazing and watering space, and there are impressive head-on forehead clashes between bulls. Supporting the mighty horizontally swung horns is a much-inflated bony skull area, the *boss*. Fibrous horn growth spreads over the boss.

Relatively poor vision attests the buffalo's forest origin. So does its reliance on water. While small herds are common in forest habitats (see page 12), savanna and plains buffalo herds often are large. The

scattered herds spread over a large area are in fact one large dispersed herd. Danger or dry-season grazing conditions cause such herds to break up into smaller herds, each with a stable female grouping.

Herd bulls, one or two massive beasts whose dominance is established and whose mating rights are assured through hierarchical interactions among males, move through the herd. Other bulls give way.

The cows are brown compared to the glossy black bulls. Their lighter horns lack the heavy downsweep and massive center boss of the males' horns.

Calves have a long period of dependency, and the bond between cow and calf is strong. Mingling in the middle of the herd, calves have security. Bleating from a calf that cannot keep up or is in distress brings the herd to the rescue. Until they are two years old, calves stay near their mothers. It is this persistent association of mother and offspring that is the basic unit of buffalo social organization. Young females remain in the herd. Presumably some males rejoin their mothers' herd after living for a time in bachelor groups or on the herd's periphery.

Buffaloes graze large areas of tall, coarse grass, pushing their wide muzzles beneath tough top growth to bite off green sprouts and tram-

pling the stems. Cattle egrets perch on broad black backs and stalk alongside, snatching insects stirred up as the buffaloes graze. During the dry season herds straggle along riverbanks to feed on clumps of tall grasses left by hippos. Midday finds buffaloes sheltering in thickets, more for protection than for shade. Wallowing is part of a buffalo's life. Much of the day is often spent immersed in the mud of a riverbank or water hole, cudding and digesting grass consumed during the early morning.

Alcelaphines

The *alcelaphines* are large ungulates derived from the gazellelike antelopes. Their horns are variously developed, but tend to be thicker at their bases, where blows are taken in horn-clashing combat. The *damaliscines* (the so-called bastard hartebeests—topi and blesbok) have horns of the enlarged gazelline kind, double-bent, mildly convex, and then concave. Impala and hirola have longer horns of the same kind, with increased curvature and wider spread.

With increased horn splay comes need for forehead protection. Wildebeests, or gnus, have evolved thick forehead bosses and a lateral sweep to horns that are recurved at the tip. The true hartebeests have frontal sinuses inflated and frontal bones enlarged to form a bony *pedicel,* or basal support, for their horns, which gives their faces a long, straight profile. Hartebeest horns, united at their bases, have heavy, upright stems that are precision weapons in head-to-head combat. Because horn support and fighting tactics require a short, thick neck, the alcelaphines get their needed reach for grazing from their lengthened faces.

Rump-stretching, gestural posturing that calls attention to the hindquarters, occurs among some of the alcelaphines. When females or young individuals assume this stance, with head lowered and hind legs stretched behind them, it functions as a turnoff to an aggressive territorial male. But a male hartebeest, with head up to display his horns and rump stretched, advertises both his aggression and the attraction of his pale colored, tail-switching hind end.

The alcelaphines are tolerant of sun and heat, but they are dependent on water or moist vegetation and cannot live in extremely arid areas. Different feeding habits preclude competition within the group. The impala, an inhabitant of woodland-grassland margins, is a sometime browser that prefers grass. The gnus are short-grass grazers. Topi and hartebeests feed on tall, coarse-stemmed grasses.

Impala

These three-toned russet antelopes are gazellelike in appearance. They are found in bush as well as plains, most often inhabiting marginal-strip habitats between open grassland and denser woodland. Dependence on good browse and water makes their distribution uneven, but where impala occur their herds are large.

Only the males have horns, slender and lyre-shaped. Their behavior is a mixture of territoriality and dominance, but their territories are poorly defined and shift about as female herds move through the area. Their herding attempts are constantly interrupted by challenges from other males.

The leaping and scattering of impalas through the bush appear to

be panic reaction and confusion. Leaps are three meters (9.8 feet) or more high and eleven meters (36 feet) or more in length. Often the hind legs give a powerful backward kick as front hoofs make their double-beat touchdown. These prodigious leaps are directed toward others in the herd. Each impala side jumps, one way and then the other, leaping over or cutting in front of each other. This casting back and forth establishes a direction of running and facilitates regrouping after the initial explosion of impalas.

In dense cover, however, it may be olfactory clues, released by fetlock glands, that maintain contact. These glands, marked by black, expand during leaping to form a scent trail that is easily followed through the bush by other impalas. Quite possibly airborne puffs of this scent keep a fleeing herd together.

Topi

Topi are beautiful antelopes with glossy, chestnut-red hides and boldly contrasting bluish-gray slashes on face, shoulders, and hind-quarters. Where rainfall and flooding produce good grazing they often form immense herds. In southwestern Uganda, near Ishasha, where ungulate species are few in number, topi are the dominant grazers. With as many as 50 topi per square kilometer (just over one-half square mile), their herds reach maximum density. Such a population peak is followed, when rains fail and grazing conditions are poor, by a crash.

The topi's preference for green-leaved grazing leads to seasonal use of habitats in the Serengeti. In the woodlands, where small herds have year-round home ranges, topi occupy the hartebeest's niche. They move from dry-season long-grass habitats to wet-season medium-grass areas on hills and ridges. Out on the plains, herds are nomadic, and topi move long distances in search of good grass.

This variance in food and habitat use is reflected in social organization. A system of female herds and territorial males prevails in the woodlands, where a male topi's territory is large enough to contain a female herd. Not only does the male defend his territory by scent-marking and visual displays, but the females are aggressive toward other topi that appear. A different way of life exists among topi on the plains, where herds, often large, consist of territorial males as well as females. During the wet-season breeding period the dominant males occupy the small territories that, during the rest of the year, they visit only now and then to scent-mark. Each topi bull herds and courts the females as they move through his territory. In short, the social organization of plains-living topi resembles that of the wildebeest.

Topi habitually stand on termite mounds, to keep watch or to enjoy cooling breezes that dispel annoying flies. For a male topi it is also assertion of territory. The sharpened angle of his body, with forequarters conspicuously higher than hindquarters, increases his vertical presence.

Belonging to the damaliscine or bastard hartebeest group, topi differ from true hartebeests by having a less elongate head and horns that are not united at their bases. Topi skirmishes involve head-on ramming and clashing of horns that now and again catch and lock in their open V.

A smaller southern African relative is the blesbok, named for its distinctive white-blazed face. Like topi, blesbok gallop with neck arched and chin tucked in, and make spectacular stiff-legged bouncing leaps.

Hirola

The hirola, or Hunter's hartebeest, has long, lyre-shaped horns, a white chevron on its forehead, a sandy-red coat color, and a white tail. A noticeable fold of skin behind its small horn pedicel allows the white-lined ears, much used in communication among these antelopes, increased mobility.

Small herds (usually 10 to 25) are found on grassy plain and bushland areas of northern Kenya and southern Somalia. Herds tend to stay in one place. Adult males are territorial. Hartebeests are grazing competitors. Their grazing companions are plains zebras, oryxes, and sometimes topi.

In some respects the hirola is impalalike; in other ways it is more like topi and hartebeest. It appears to be a relic population of an antelope that once had a wide distribution. A larger, more massive hirolalike antelope has been recovered at Olduvai Gorge in Tanzania, from Pleistocene deposits laid down more than a million years ago.

Hartebeest

Sloping backs and very long faces topped by a bony pedicel characterize the hartebeests. Their bodies are deep-chested and hump-shouldered (because of long spines on the thoracic vertebrae). Their legs are relatively long and slender. A fringe of stiff black hairs makes their tails elegant fly whisks. Horns vary in size and shape from nubbins on a month-old calf to the straight-forked horn set of a yearling to the heavily ridged, double-curved, hooked horns, V-shaped at their base, of the adult.

On each side of the hartebeest's rump a line is formed where darker body color gives way to a light-tawny rump color. This demarcation coincides with the extent of head reach. Hartebeests, highly social, have the habit of marking their shoulders, back, and flanks with secretion from a facial gland just below each eye. They also use this preorbital-gland secretion to mark stumps, termitaries, and grass stems. Then they rub their foreheads against the marked object. Territorial males thus become standing or moving scent posts.

Herds of 6 to 20 graze in morning and again in late afternoon. Cattle egrets are sometimes feeding companions. Nearby a hartebeest stands sentinel on a termite mound. When a predator is detected by sight and smell, the sentry gives a loud sneeze-snort and the herd gallops off in single file. First one and then all of them begin pronking, or stotting. This bouncing, stiff-legged gait, used by many of the antelopes, small as well as large, is ritualized leaping that invites imitation and probably serves to keep herd members together. Usually it occurs at the beginning of a chase or at the end. Pronking also inhibits predators. Neck up and head high, their legs as stiff as ramrods, the hartebeests spring up and down.

Female hartebeests form loose associations. Often they are seen with two or three generations of their offspring. A cow with a very young calf hidden in grass or thicket relies on pronking to distract and lure away any passing predator.

By their third year males are driven off and form bachelor groups. In these small herds, contests for dominance are frequent as males begin the changeover from nonterritorial to territorial lifestyle. A dominant male often asserts his status by standing atop a termitary, the other males clustered below him.

When challenged on his territory, a bull walks toward the intruder

with exaggerated nods of his long head, showing off his horns in profile. Sometimes a fight ensues.

The fawn-colored Coke's hartebeest, or kongoni, occurs in the grasslands and wooded savannas of southern Kenya and the northern half of Tanzania. Jackson's (or Lelwel's) hartebeest is taller, reddish in color with dark markings on legs and sometimes on its face, and a very high horn pedicel. It is found in grassland areas of Uganda, and in Kenya and Tanzania near Lake Victoria. Lichtenstein's hartebeest lives in bush and wooded grassland habitats of Tanzania.

129   The Grasslands

Wildebeest

With its long, black face, Roman-nosed profile, oxlike horns, white beard, humped shoulders, sloping back, and horselike hindquarters, the wildebeest (or white-bearded gnu) is well endowed to play the fool. This it does whenever approached. First this silvery gray bovid, brindled with vertical bands of brown on neck and shoulders, stands and stares or trots sideways, spooking, honking, and wheezing. Then, with a flick of its black tail, it spins about and gallops away, bucking and plunging, head down and tail lashing.

Of all the gnus, the white-tailed is the most frolicsome. Also known as the black wildebeest, it is dark brown to black, has upward-curving horns, bristly hair tufts on face, throat, and chest, and a long, flowing white tail. Nearly exterminated by hunters for meat and hides, it is now restricted to parks and reserves in southern Africa.

Gregarious to a degree unmatched by any other ungulates, wildebeest are grazers of the short-grass plains and open savannas. Their wanderings depend upon availability of water and grazing. During the wet season, huge wandering herds disperse across a green and growing grassland. When the dry season comes, vast herds move through open savanna-woodland areas where there is water and grass.

In the Serengeti, wildebeest migrations are regular. Annually the herds move between the short-grass plains in the east, where they stay from January through April or May, and dry-season areas to the west and then north into the Mara, where they remain until November or December.

Over this 12,000-square-mile area wildebeest herds, often numbering in the thousands, move in response to rain. Somehow they sense where it is falling, detecting it as far as 30 miles away. They move toward the rain, following a network of well-defined trails.

Actually wildebeests are always on the move, for better grazing and watering places. It is only in certain years that their migrations are spectacular. Then, when conditions are just right, long columns of wildebeests, heads low and plodding one after the other, file across the plains.

Wildebeests graze like lawnmowers, literally mowing their way over the grassland. Their wide, flat, muscular lips press grass leaves into their mouths, cutting them against a row of sharp lower incisor teeth. Often they cluster to graze in a particular place, now and again rubbing against each other. When they rest they stand rumps touching, or lie down back to back.

Males leave their mothers' herds as yearlings. They live for two or three years in bachelor groups, then become solitary before attempting to take over a territory. In Ngorongoro Crater, where Richard D. Estes observed wildebeests, the dominant adult males maintain permanent territories, typical alcelaphine behavior.

Social organization is restricted in the very large herds in the Serengeti. *Rut* (mating time) comes as the wildebeests are moving off the plains. The bulls, their hormone levels high, suddenly become intolerant of each other. During grazing interludes they grunt loudly and push at one another to stake out their small temporary territories, usually located near a tree or termite mound.

On his territory the bull displays his dominance by dashing in circles, kicking and bucking. A bare patch at the center is his stomping ground, where he spends much of his time. It is marked by his urine, manure, horn-rubbing and face-rubbing, and rolling. Stiff, black facial hairs form a bristly scent brush that dispenses secretion from his preorbital glands. When challenged by another male, the bull canters rocking-horse style, head up and tail swishing, to meet his adversary. At the peak of mating time the herding and chasing of females and the grunting and tussling encounters with other males often cause a frenzied bull to foam at the mouth.

Calving, some eight to nine months later, is a wet-season occurrence. Within two or three weeks (November to January in southern Africa and in January and February in the Serengeti) hundreds of thousands of wildebeest cows drop their calves. This synchronization of births shortens the period when calves are most vulnerable. At calving time cows move into the center of the herd. Even though there is some safety in numbers, loss to predators is high.

Within minutes, the newborn light-brownish-colored calf is up. Its mother moves between her wobbly offspring and attendant jackals that dart in to snatch the afterbirth. The calf quickly tries out its long, spindly legs. Coordination comes within an hour. Then the calf can run at its mother's side and, most importantly, not become lost in the confusion of the herd. At ten days the calf starts to crop grass. Soon it joins a play group, to butt, chase, and pronk with other calves.

Zebras Zebras, like their odd-toed relatives the rhinos, live on grassy plains or in open scrub country. While rhinos have three toes, zebras have only one functional digit. These *equids* (members of the horse family, Equidae) walk, trot, canter, and gallop on their toe tips. The horny hoof of each foot encases and is supported by the enlarged spadelike end-bone of the third digit (finger or toe). Digits two and four are reduced to sliverlike splint bones that lie along the lower leg bone.

High-crowned cheek teeth, each a four-columned grinding structure with cement infoldings, equip zebras for grazing. Grass, silica-containing and abrasive, causes continual wear. To maintain grinding position, the open-rooted teeth push up or down out of the jaws throughout the zebra's lifespan.

Because food intake passes rapidly through their simple-stomach digestive system, zebras require almost twice as much grass as do their ruminant relatives (antelopes, sheep, goats). Their less-efficient

digestive tract, however, allows them a slimmer barrel contour and a weight distribution that is better adapted for running. Not only do zebras consume larger quantities, but they will feed on all kinds and parts of grasses and can survive in dry, barren areas where tough grasses grow in scattered clumps.

These striped horses of Africa are of three kinds, each species readily distinguished by body size, ear size and shape, and stripe patterns.

Grévy's Zebra

Grévy's zebra, found in northern Kenya, as well as in parts of Somalia and southeastern Ethiopia, is the tallest of the zebras. It is long legged and has large, heavily haired, rounded ears, a long, narrow head, a profusion of long *vibrissae* (whiskers) on its brown muzzle, and a close-set pattern of narrow stripes. Vertical to the *croup* (point of rump), the stripes form a triple-arch pattern on each side of the hindquarters and a concentric pattern around the root of the tail. The broad spinal stripe, widest along mid-back, is bordered by white. Legs are banded to the hooves.

This is the zebra that once was killed by proud Galla tribesmen, who took its black-and-white mane to embellish the necks of their own horses. Grévy's zebras, pulling ceremonial carts, were also seen in the circuses of ancient Rome. The last of the zebras to gain scientific recognition, it was named in 1882 for the President of France, Jules Grévy.

Grévy's zebras move about in changing seasonal and group associations. Their social life is very different from that of the other zebras. Stallions (six years and older) have territories for part of the

year. Mares with their foals form loosely structured nursery bands. There are also large mixed herds and bachelor groups of younger males. Territorial stallions, their landholdings marked by dung piles and spaced over large areas, assert their dominance over males moving through with arched neck and high leg action. A subordinate male approaches with lowered head and extended tail to nuzzle the territory holder. Unless an estrous mare is nearby, territorial stallions are tolerant of itinerant males and even appear to seek their grazing company.

A Grévy's foal is striped reddish brown, its wispy mane and tail connected by a dark dorsal band of coarse hairs. When the foal is frightened or excited, these hairs stand up. They are also the focus for its mother's nibbling and rubbing and therefore important in the maintaining of the mare-foal bond. Mares with new foals tend to avoid large grazing herds and form small nursing groups. About the fourth month, in head-to-tail progression, darker brown-black hairs replace the reddish ones, and short hairs replace the longer-haired baby coat. But the wide black portion of the dorsal stripe, from croup to tail root, remains conspicuous, a mark that will be useful in single-file travel throughout a zebra's life.

Mountain Zebra

In arid, stony mountains and foothills of southwestern Angola, Namibia, and parts of South Africa live mountain zebras. Small and narrow-bodied, with long, pointed ears, their characteristics include a

conspicuous dewlap and a pattern of vertical body stripes that connect with the spinal stripe but do not extend onto the white belly. Broad stripes extend horizontally over the hindquarters. A gridiron pattern is formed by short transverse stripes on the rump. Legs are banded to the steep, narrow hoofs.

Rocky hillsides are the refuge of mountain zebras. There they graze on tufts of grass and rest under thornbushes during midday. They can go for several days without water. In dry stream beds they

sniff out pools beneath the sand and gravel, then with their front hoofs paw drinking holes.

When frightened, mountain zebras run uphill, galloping for a distance, then dropping to a ground-covering trot. Unlike the other zebras they do not circle, stop, and look back.

Plains Zebra

Plains (or Burchell's) zebras have patterns of striping that vary in a north-to-south trend in their overlapping populations. Bold striping and complete (to-the-hoof) leg banding mark zebras of eastern and central Africa. Further south, striping and leg banding diminish. In southern Africa zebras tend toward uniform coloration. Brownish shadow stripes are developed in between wide, black flank stripes and on some, the color of the interspaces is darker. Others have incompletely striped bodies. The high veld of South Africa was home to a race of zebra that had a nearly white rump and white legs and belly, a reduction of striping sometimes seen today among zebras in Zululand and in the western Kalahari.

The end point in this trend was the quagga, an extinct zebra of the Karroo, a desert region near the tip of South Africa. Its chestnut-colored body had dark, reddish-brown stripes only on head, neck, and shoulders. Its belly, legs, and tail were creamy white. Relentlessly slaughtered by Boer farmers and trekkers who used their hides for sacks and shoe leather and their meat to feed their Hottentot servants, quaggas were exterminated in the early 1860s. The last quagga, a mare in the Amsterdam Zoo, died in 1883.

Like mountain zebras, plains zebras live in family groups, a stallion with one to several mares and their foals. There are also bachelor bands. Mares represent a stallion's movable territory. He is possessive of his harem. Zebras move freely through large home ranges, the extent of their wanderings depending upon ecological conditions.

Where lush grazing causes large herds to form, family units maintain contact. If alarm results in a wheeling stampede and the herd gallops away in a confusion of stripes and braying barks, the families sort themselves out. Each family group bunches together, the stallion bringing up the rear. When necessary he drops behind and turns on pursuing predators.

Zebra families are stable units, mares usually living out their lives in the same group. A stallion's life is more precarious. He is tireless in his efforts to keep his family together, herding the mares and oc-

casionally searching for a mare and foal that have been separated from the group. As he ages his role is usurped by a younger stallion.

An estrous filly often is the cause for a fight between zebra stallions. After trying to bite each other's legs, the stallions rear to battle with bare teeth, flailing forelegs, and thudding, thumping hoofs. Mares and foals stand by restlessly, waiting to see the outcome. Sooner or later one stallion gives up and turns tail. With a few well-aimed kicks that discourage the victor's pursuit, the contest ends.

Epilogue

Africa, with its vast skies and far-off horizons, evokes a sense of wildness, freedom, and wonder. It is a land that echoes the past, where natural order prevails and days are without time.

A coterie of cattle egrets rises and settles again on the broad, twitching, dust-covered backs of grazing buffalo. Wildebeests, white beards blowing and black tail tassels hanging on the wind, plod steadfastly across the plains, headed for a distant thunderstorm. Wild dogs with bat ears and gaunt bodies pirouette in play. Zebras file along the skyline, veer suddenly, then mill together, flank pressed against flank and ears pricked. Lions lie deep in tawny grass. A leopard drapes in sun-spotted shade along the limb of a fever tree, while from a nearby crotch swings the hollow form of a gazelle.

In the delicate springlike shade of an acacia, a gerenuk browses, its tail switching, ears batting, and front hoofs propped among the branches. A tiny dik-dik with enormous mouselike eyes ringed in white stares shyly from a thicket. A bull elephant threatens, flaring huge veined ears, brandishing tusks, testing with trunk, and swinging his pendulumlike foreleg sideways.

These are among the images of Africa, glimpses of its varied and beautiful landscapes and the array of animals that live in grassland, savanna, bush, and forest.

ABOUT THE ARTIST

UGO MOCHI (1889–1977) devoted much of his life to the study of animals. A keen observer of character, gesture, and action in animals, Mochi worked with black paper and a small lithographer's knife, flawlessly interpreting form with a sculptural simplicity. Each image (cutout or, as he preferred to call it, graphic sculpture) is an expression of the artist's sensitive feeling for the essential being of the animal depicted. Accuracy of outline attests his thorough grasp of the underlying complexity of each animal's bones, muscles, and nerves.

The awe, delight, and enthusiasm Ugo Mochi found in the beauty and diversity of animal forms animates his subjects. Some of his animals in outline display a tense, nervous energy. Others rest, flee, or fight. Their forms, emphasized against large areas of negative space, suggest distance and evoke mood.

While Ugo Mochi's animal images are accurate enough to satisfy a scientist's critical eye, their striking designs also please the artist. Ugo Mochi was indeed the master of his medium.

List of Animals in Outline

Mammals

Insectivora
  Macroscelididae
    Elephant shrew, *Elephantulus rufescens*

Primates
  Pongidae (apes)
    Gorilla, *Gorilla gorilla*
    Chimpanzee, *Pan troglodytes*
  Cercopithecidae (Old World monkeys)
    Black-and-white colobus, *Colobus abyssinicus*
    Baboon, *Papio cynocephalus*
    Mandrill, *Papio mandrillus*
    Drill, *Papio leucophaeus*

Tubulidentata
  Orycteropidae
    Aardvark, *Orycteropus afer*

Rodentia
  Pedetidae
    Springhare, *Pedetes capensis*
  Hystricidae (Old World porcupines)
    African porcupine, *Hystrix cristata*
    Brush-tailed porcupine, *Atherurus africanus*
  Muridae (rats and mice)
    Spiny mouse, *Acomys subspinosus*

Carnivora
  Canidae (canids)
    Golden jackal, *Canis aureus*
    Black-backed jackal, *Canis mesomelas*
    African wild dog, *Lycaon pictus*
    Bat-eared fox, *Otocyon megalotis*
  Viverridae (viverrids)
    Blotched genet, *Genetta tigrina*
    African civet, *Civettictis civetta*
    African mongoose, *Herpestes ichneumon*
  Hyaenidae (hyaenids)
    Spotted hyena, *Crocuta crocuta*
    Aardwolf, *Proteles cristatus*
  Felidae (felids)
    Serval, *Felis serval*
    Caracal, *Felis caracal*
    Leopard, *Felis (Panthera) pardus*
    Lion, *Felis (Panthera) leo*
    Cheetah, *Acinonyx jubatus*

Proboscidea
  Elephantidae (elephants)
    African elephant, *Loxodonta africana*

Perissodactyla (odd-toed hoofed mammals)
  Rhinocerotidae (rhinoceroses)
    Black rhino, *Diceros bicornis*
    White rhino, *Ceratotherium simum*

Equidae (equids)
    Grévy's zebra, *Equus grevyi*
    Mountain zebra, *Equus zebra*
    Plains zebra, *Equus burchelli*
Artiodactyla (even-toed hoofed mammals)
    Suidae (pigs)
        Bushpig, *Potamochoerus porcus*
        Giant forest hog, *Hylochoerus meinertzhageni*
        Warthog, *Phacochoerus aethiopicus*
    Hippopotamidae
        Hippopotamus, *Hippopotamus amphibius*
    Tragulidae (chevrotains)
        Water chevrotain, *Hyemoschus aquaticus*
    Giraffidae
        Giraffe, *Giraffa camelopardalis*
        Okapi, *Okapia johnstoni*
Bovidae (horned ungulates)
    Bovinae (bovines)
        Bovini (oxen)
            African buffalo, *Syncerus caffer*
        Tragelaphini (tragelaphines)
            Sitatunga, *Tragelaphus spekei*
            Bushbuck, *Tragelaphus scriptus*
            Lesser kudu, *Tragelaphus imberbis*
            Greater kudu, *Tragelaphus strepsiceros*
            Eland, *Tragelaphus oryx*
            Bongo, *Boocercus eurycerus*
            Nyala, *Tragelaphus angasi*
            Mountain nyala, *Tragelaphus buxtoni*
    Antilopinae
        Neotragini (dwarf antelopes)
            Klipspringer, *Oreotragus oreotragus*
            Dik-dik, *Madoqua kirki*
        Cephalophini (duikers)
            Red duiker, *Cephalophus harveyi*

Reduncini (reduncines)
    Bohor reedbuck, *Redunca redunca*
    Kob, *Kobus kob*
    Waterbuck, *Kobus ellipsiprymnus*
Antilopini (gazelline antelopes)
    Thomson's gazelle, *Gazella thomsoni*
    Grant's gazelle, *Gazella granti*
    Gerenuk, *Litocranius walleri*
Alcelaphini (alcelaphines)
    Impala, *Aepyceros melampus*
    Hirola, Hunter's hartebeest, *Beatragus hunteri*
    Topi, blesbok, *Damaliscus lunatus*
    Hartebeest, kongoni, *Alcelaphus buselaphus*
    Wildebeest, *Connochaetes taurinus*
    White-tailed gnu, *Connochaetes gnou*
Hippotragini (hippotragines)
    Sable antelope, *Hippotragus niger*
    Roan antelope, *Hippotragus equinus*
    Oryx, *Oryx gazella*

Birds

Ostrich, *Struthio camelus*
Pelican, *Pelecanus* sp.
Goliath heron, *Ardea goliath*
Buff-backed heron or cattle egret, *Bubulcus ibis*
Whale-headed stork, *Balaeniceps rex*
Marabou stork, *Leptoptilos crumeniferus*
Greater flamingo, *Phoeniconaias ruber*
Lesser flamingo, *Phoeniconaias minor*
Secretary bird, *Sagittarius serpentarius*
Ruppell's griffon vulture, *Gyps ruppelli*
Bateleur eagle, *Terathopius ecaudatus*

Helmeted guinea fowl, *Numida mitrata*
Crowned crane, *Balearica regulorum*
African jacana or lily-trotter, *Actophilornis africanus*
Spur-wing plover, *Hoplopterus spinosus*
Casqued hornbill, *Bycanistes* sp.
Ground hornbill, *Bucorvus leadbeateri*

Speckled mousebird, *Colius striatus*
Red-billed oxpecker, *Buphagus erythorhynchus*

Reptiles

Nile crocodile, *Crocodylus niloticus*

Glossary

ALCELAPHINES. Antelopes of the tribe Alcelaphini that live in large herds on the open plains; wildebeest, hartebeest, kongoni, blesbok, hirola, impala

AUDITORY BULLAE. Paired, thin-walled, bony chambers of the skull beneath the opening of the ear

BIPEDAL. Having two feet, an adjective used to describe animals that locomote by hopping or leaping on their hind legs

BOSS. Rounded protuberance formed by horns that are flattened and thick at the base

BOVID. A member of the family Bovidae, which includes antelopes, gazelles, and the African buffalo

BROWSE. As a noun, the shoots, leaves, and twigs of shrubs and trees

BROWSE. A verb meaning to feed on leaves and twigs

CANIDS. Members of the dog family, the Canidae

CARNIVORES. Mammals of the order Carnivora, most of them largely carnivorous or meat-eating

CROUP. In hoofed mammals, the part of the back above the hind legs

CURSORIAL. Adapted for running

DAMALISCINE. A term used to describe antelopes of the genus *Damaliscus:* topi, blesbok, and hirola

DENTITION. The type, number, and arrangement of teeth

DEWLAP. A pendant skin fold on underside of neck

DISPLAY. An inherited behavior pattern, usually associated with courtship or territorial defense, which involves ritualized posturing

DONGAS. Narrow, ditchlike stream beds, often tree- or shrub-lined, of savanna and bush country; dry during much of the year, they flashflood when the rains come

ECOLOGY. The science of the relationships between plants and animals and their environments

EQUIDS. Members of the horse family, the Equidae, which includes zebras, as well as horses and asses

ESTRUS. A period in the reproductive cycle of the female when she is most receptive physiologically and psychologically to the male

ESTROUS. An adjective describing the condition of estrus

ETHOLOGIST. A scientist who studies animal behavior

FELIDS. Carnivores that belong to the cat family, the Felidae

GAZELLINE. Gazellelike, referring to gerenuks and the gazelles

HABITAT. The area or type of environment in which an animal (or plant) lives

HERBIVORES. Animals that feed on plants

HIPPOTRAGINES. The horselike antelopes of the tribe Hippotragini, sable, roan, and oryx

HOME RANGE. The area over which an animal roams in the course of its normal activities

HYAENIDS. Carnivores of the family Hyaenidae; hyenas and aardwolf

IMPRINTING. The formation of a close relationship, or bond, between mother and newborn

INSECTIVORES. Mammals of the order Insectivora, small terrestrial, nocturnal insect-eaters

KOPJES. "Islands" of boulders, weathered granite and gneiss, that stud the Serengeti plains and other grassland areas

LEK. An area used consistently for group courtship displays

MANDIBLE. Jaw, either upper or lower in birds and other animals that have a beak, but in mammals usually meaning the lower jaw

MATRILINE. Female descent, from mother to offspring

MBUGAS. Broad, grassy valleys that flood during the wet season

MIOMBO. The wood savannas from southern Tanzania and Mozambique to southern Zaire and Angola

NOCTURNAL. Active at night

NYIKA. The bushlands of East Africa

OMNIVORE. An animal that eats both animal and plant materials

PAIR BONDING. A close, long-lasting association between a male and female, formed primarily for cooperative rearing of young

PELAGE. The hairy, furry, wooly, or spiny coat of a mammal

PEDICEL. Upper part of the skull that supports the horn cores of some alcelaphine antelopes

PREDATOR. An animal that kills and eats other animals

PREHENSILE. Adapted for wrapping around and grasping

PREORBITAL GLAND. A gland at the inner corner of the eye of some antelopes whose secretion is used for marking territory or each other

PREY. A living animal that is captured for food by another animal

PRIDE. A family or social group of lions

PROBOSCIS. A long, flexible snout

PRONKING. A bouncing, stiff-legged gait in which all hoofs hit the ground at the same time; also stotting, or spronking

RAPTORS. Birds of prey: hawks, eagles, vultures, and owls

REDUNCINES. Antelopes of the tribe Reduncini, grazers that live in marshes or near water: waterbuck, kob, reedbuck

RHINARIUM. The naked-skinned nose pad of carnivores and some other mammals

RUMINANT. A mammal that ruminates, or chews its cud

RUT. The period of estrus in certain antelopes and other bovids

SALTATORIAL. Adapted for hopping or leaping

SAVANNA. A landscape dominated by grasses with widely scattered, small-leafed, thorny trees

SCAVENGERS. Carrion-eaters, animals that feed on dead or decaying flesh

SOUNDER. A family group of warthogs or other members of the pig family

STOTTING. See pronking

TERMITARIES. Pillarlike mounds, constructed of soil, saliva, and other secretions, which are nests of termites

TERRITORY. An area occupied more or less exclusively by an animal or group of animals, from which others of the same species are excluded by defensive behavior or by marking

TRAGELAPHINES. Antelopes of the tribe Tragelaphini, most of them inhabitants of forest or bush, with stripes or spots on the body, a white chevron on the forehead, and a spinal crest of hairs: bongo, sitatunga, bushbuck, lesser kudu, greater kudu, nyala, mountain nyala, and eland

TROOP. A group of monkeys or apes

TRYPANOSOMES. One-celled blood parasites that cause the disease trypanosomiasis

UNGULATES. Hoofed animals, including the odd-toed perissodactyls (rhinos and zebras) and the even-toed artiodactyls (hippo, the wild pigs, giraffe and okapi, the antelopes and gazelles, and African buffalo)

VIBRISSAE. Stiff hairs or whiskers of muzzle, tactile in function

VIVERRIDS. Small- to medium-sized carnivores, most of them forest or bush dwellers, with elongated bodies and pointed muzzles: civets, genets, and mongooses

Further Reading

Many observers of animal life in Africa have written accounts of their experiences in the field, in addition to having published their findings in scientific journals. Their books supply firsthand information on animals that may be of special interest to the reader.

Jonathan Kingdon's seven volumes contain a wealth of details on behavior and anatomy, complimented by superb gestural sketches and anatomical drawings. Cynthia Moss, an elephant researcher, gives a most readable account of behavior studies of 15 of Africa's animals.

Also included are several books about Africa and a few articles with photographs about specific animals.

Brown, Leslie. *The Life of the African Plains.* New York: McGraw-Hill Book Co., 1972.

Carr, Archie. *The Land and Wildlife of Africa.* New York: Time Inc., 1964.

Cott, Hugh B. *Looking at Animals.* New York: Charles Scribner's Sons, 1975.

Dagg, Anne Innis and Foster, J. Bristol. *The Giraffe.* New York: Van Nostrand Reinhold Co., 1976.

Douglas-Hamilton, Iaian and Oria. *Among the Elephants.* New York: The Viking Press, 1975.

Estes, Richard D. "Sable by Moonlight." *Animal Kingdom,* August–September, 1983, pp. 10–16.

Fossey, Dian. *Gorillas in the Mist.* Boston: Houghton Mifflin Co., 1983.

Frame, George and Lory. *Swift and Enduring.* Cheetahs and Wild Dogs of the Serengeti. New York: E.P. Dutton, 1981.

Goodall, Jane and van Lawick, Hugo. *Innocent Killers.* Boston: Houghton Mifflin Co., 1971.

Hanby, Jeannette and Bygott, David. *Lions Share*. Boston: Houghton Mifflin Co., 1982.

Kingdon, Jonathan. *East African Mammals*. 7 vols. New York: Academic Press, 1971–1982.

Kruuk, Hans. *Hyaena*. London: Oxford University Press, 1975.

MacClintock, Dorcas and Mochi, Ugo. *A Natural History of Giraffes*. New York: Charles Scribner's Sons, 1973.

————. *A Natural History of Zebras*. New York: Charles Scribner's Sons, 1976.

Martin, Esmund Bradley. *Run, Rhino, Run*. London: Chatto and Windus Ltd., 1982.

Mochi, Ugo and Carter, T. Donald. *Hoofed Mammals of the World*. New York: Charles Scribner's Sons, 1971.

Moehlman, Patricia D. "Jackals of the Serengeti." *National Geographic* 158 (1980): pp. 840–850.

Moss, Cynthia. *Portraits in the Wild*. Chicago: The University of Chicago Press, 1982.

Myers, Norman. *The Long African Day*. New York: The Macmillan Co., 1972.

Schaller, George B. *Golden Shadows, Flying Hooves*. New York: Alfred A. Knopf, 1973.

Index

termite mounds *(cont.)*
 108, 109, 110, 112, 124, 127, 132, 149
territory, xii; civet, 90; dik-dik, 49; duiker, 5; gazelle, 114; gerenuk, 58–59; hartebeest, 127, 128; hippo, 31; hyena, 94; jackal, 86; klipspringer, 26; leopard, 102; lion, 99; reedbuck 38; sable, 67–68; topi, 123; waterbuck, 36; wildebeest, 132; zebra (Grévy's), 135
thermoregulation: crocodile, 35; dik-dik, 49; eland, 78; giraffe, 74; hippo, 33; oryx, 64
topi, 38, 109, 121, 123–124, 145
Treetops, 4
troops, 150; baboon, 19; colobus monkey, 34; chimpanzee, 15; gorilla, 13; vervet monkey, 17
trypanosomes, 69, 150
Tsavo (East and West) National Parks (Kenya), 53, 54, 58–59
tsetse flies, 69
turaco, 2, 17

U
Uganda, 1, 7, 15, 34, 70, 71, 109, 111, 123, 129

V
vervet monkey, 17
Victoria, Lake, 129
Virunga Mountains, 14
viverrids, 89–92, 144, 150
vulture, 86, 92, 105–107, 145

W
warthog, 10, 32, 80–81, 102, 145
waterbuck, 35–37, 66, 145
wild dog, 37, 63, 78, 84–85, 87–88, 101, 112, 116, 140, 144
wildebeest, 85, 87, 93–94, 97, 109, 115, 130–133, 140, 145

Z
Zaire, 1, 14, 66, 76, 111
Zambesi River, 22
zebra, xiii, 66, 85, 88, 93, 97, 103, 109, 115, 117, 133–134; Grévy's, 134–135, 145; mountain, 135–137, 145; plains (or Burchell's), 137–139, 145
Zululand, 137